WHITE STAR PUBLISHERS

Smoothies
& Juices

HEALTH AND ENERGY IN A GLASS

INTRODUCTION AND IN-DEPTH ARTICLES
Maurizio Cusani

PHOTOGRAPHS AND RECIPES
Cinzia Trenchi

PREFACE

by Cinzia Trenchi

To prepare a smoothie you need neither to pass a lot of time in the kitchen at the expense of other commitments, family and work, nor to attend any particular courses. It is sufficient to supply yourself with a blender and the deal is done: just a handful of seconds and the pulp of fruit and vegetables can be transformed into many delicious, smooth and creamy beverages that are extremely appetizing and soft-textured! Juices require a slightly more complex procedure if they exclude fruit such as oranges, mandarin oranges, grapefruit and lemons, for which a simple lemon juicer is sufficient. Vegetables, on the other hand, require a juicing press, centrifugal juicer or a utensil that can separate the solid portion of the vegetable from the liquid.

On the market, you can find anything. There is a wealth of options to choose from however, there are some simple considerations that must be kept in mind in order to choose the best domestic appliance: processing should be performed at a speed that is not too excessive, which can damage foods; and juice extraction should not be too violent or occur at temperatures that are too high. Finally, the price of the appliance, which should correspond to your expectations, should be carefully considered. Once this obstacle is overcome, just let your imagination run or follow the recipes on the following pages.

Five are the sections from which to get inspiration for many inviting preparations: fruit juices, emulsions and smoothies; vegetable juices, emulsions and smoothies; mixed juices, emulsions and smoothies (with combinations of fruit and vegetables); juices, emulsions and smoothies with vegetable proteins (vegan); and juices, emulsions and smoothies with animal proteins.

Easy recipes where color, flavor and simplicity unite to create excellent beverages flavored with spices, aromatic herbs and at times, oil. Beverages in which the natural flavor of the ingredients blends to gift the palate satisfaction and integrate our diet with foods rich in properties useful to our wellbeing. There are many suggestions for enriching meals and snacks by allowing oneself to be guided by the seasons and using fruit and vegetables that have reached a peak maturation naturally.

TABLE OF CONTENTS

MIXED FRUIT AND VEGETABLE JUICES, EMULSIONS AND SMOOTHIES

JUICES, EMULSIONS AND SMOOTHIES
WITH VEGETABLE PROTEINS

JUICES, EMULSIONS AND SMOOTHIES WITH ANIMAL PROTEINS

INDEX

INTRODUCTION

by Maurizio Cusani

The average diet typical of the modern Western way of life is very rich in refined sugars, salt and red meat.

Consequently, there has been an exponential rise in metabolic diseases, such as diabetes and obesity, cancer and degenerative diseases, such as those involving the heart and the circulation, which is independent of increasing life expectancy. Changing one's diet to promote health is not, however, that difficult and can prove a simple and pleasant process, which has as its goal not only losing weight but also improving personal wellbeing.

How can juices, juice concentrates and smoothies help us in this sense?

We will see in more detail in the following chapters.

All of the aging processes of our organs can be linked mostly to the activities of toxic substances, which accumulate with time: for example, this is the case with free radicals, which can be effectively regulated and controlled by antioxidant nutrients assumed for the most part through our diet.

Therefore, the best type of diet for preventing disease, prolonging life, and keeping ourselves young and our skin elastic is one built around foods rich in antioxidants and low in calories. The foods most rich in these beneficial compounds are fruit, legumes and vegetables.

Cooking and long-term storage reduce the efficacy of antioxidant substances. Therefore, ideally, these foods should be consumed raw when possible; in addition, it would be best if these foods were produced in close proximity to the place of consumption.

One of the possible solutions is to return to the use of whole foods and the consumption of homemade pasta, which however often requires long preparation. But, modern priorities, driven by the limited time available to dedicate to the family, have meant that for many the time to make use of this ancient gastronomical heritage is extremely limited. An alternative, simpler and more creative solution consists in the blending of the nutraceutical compounds best

for our bodies in beverages that are easy to prepare and quick to consume, such as juices, juice concentrates and smoothies, without forgetting that our body always needs a constant and well-balanced supply of fiber, minerals, fats, sugars and proteins.

Juices, juice concentrates and smoothies are in fact capable of providing our bodies with a concentrated dose of compounds that may prove crucial to maintaining personal health, in addition to being low in calories and capable of promoting weight loss. Of course, it is necessary to carefully access each case before using such preparations, which in any case have traditionally been used in families (above all for children, the elderly and convalescents) for centuries. These beverages are becoming increasingly popular due to the simplicity of their preparation and the beneficial effects that they are capable of producing in certain conditions, and because they allow our imagination to run wild creating the most varied of blends and even bringing out the beauty and color of the products. So popular in fact, that some have even been promoting an actual "liquid diet", which certainly brings with it many advantages, such as the possibility to lose weight in a simple way while guaranteeing the wellbeing of the body.

WHAT ARE JUICES, SMOOTHIES AND EMULSIONS?

FRUIT JUICES By squeezing the fruit and consequently eliminating its more fibrous portions, we obtain fruit juices. Citrus fruit juices, on the other hand, can be easily prepared in a manual lemon juicer. The traditional freshly-squeezed orange and grapefruit juices are particularly popular, as well as those consisting of apples and pears.

Since they can prove excessively concentrated and at times unpleasant to some palates, because too sour, bitter or acidic, natural juices are often diluted with water or, in the summer, with ice.

Hence, these juices are the concentrates of individual fruit and are very different from beverages or nectars, which also contain other substances.

CENTRIFUGED JUICES   To juice all other plants it is necessary to use a centrifugal juicer; in this way we obtain centrifuged juices. Since it is common practice to prepare mixtures that combine different fruit and vegetables (tomatoes or carrots with apples or pears, for example), it is perfectly acceptable to mix natural fruit juices with vegetable juice concentrates to create original mixes. Each of us can let our imagination run wild and invent new combinations. This book is intended as a collection of suggestions and as an inspiration to create new blends.

SMOOTHIES   Smoothies are beverages in which the fibrous portions of the fruit and vegetables are retained. They provide the body with a complete series of active compounds, do a better job of regulating the digestive system with respect to other preparations, and guarantee a higher feeling of fullness.

Even though smoothies are sometimes higher in calories, the greater feeling of fullness that they provide triggers a neuro-digestive response that prevents an individual from feeling hunger pangs or sensing an empty feeling in the stomach for many hours after consumption. Hence, this reduces the need to eat, favoring any type of diet.

Depending on individual wellbeing needs, other ingredients, including milk, soy milk, egg yolk, ricotta, yogurt and many others, can be added to the smoothie.

EMULSIONS   Emulsions are dispersions of a fluid in the form of minute droplets in another fluid, called the continuous phase, with which it cannot mix, if not on an infinitesimal level.

Therefore, emulsions are defined by two phases, the dispersed phase and the dispersant, i.e. the continuous phase. One example is water and oil, where water is dispersed in oil. Another natural emulsion is milk. Emulsions that are also suitable for weight-loss diets contain ingredients such as extra virgin olive oil, egg yolk and ricotta.

COMPOSITION OF JUICES AND SMOOTHIES

HOW TO CHOOSE THE INGREDIENTS   It is useful to know how to choose the most suitable fruit and vegetables. In fact, it is very important that they are fresh, ripe and organically grown, and therefore contain the least amount of pesticides (which can get concentrated in smoothies, if skin is not removed, but also in juices, because many chemical compounds can penetrate deep into the fruit). If the ingredients are local it is even better, because in this way, less of their natural properties are lost.

To make the smoothies easier to digest and suitable to various diets, cow milk (low-fat), soy milk or yogurt (plain and low-fat) can be added.

Finally, it should always be kept in mind that juices and smoothies should be consumed while still fresh. In fact, it is best to never store them in the refrigerator because the vitamins and active ingredients they contain become less potent and loose some of their properties.

SWEETENING   Smoothies are best unsweetened, since fruit and many vegetables (such as carrots, for example) already contain many sugar compounds. In addition, smoothies composed exclusively of vegetables can be effectively flavored with spices, herbs, lemon juice and other ingredients.

For those who just cannot do without, the best sweetener is honey, if possible of domestic and hence better-regulated production (many imported honeys contain antibiotics, for example), because it blends better. Sugar is forbidden.

THE COLORS   Color is an interesting indicator. In fact, the color of fruit and vegetables signals the presence of antioxidants (and specifically, which antioxidants); hence, these foods when combined in a correct manner can produce blends that are balanced and beautiful to see, when correctly alternated. In addition, colors have always played an important role in the appeal of a food because they transmit information and sensations that influence the feelings of pleasure, or lack thereof, triggered by what we eat. Already in ancient times, color was used to enrich the table by adding an artistic touch that changed the natural appearance of foods, as it is still used today in Asian cuisines - Chinese and Japanese, for example - where the choreographic presentation of a dish and the pairing of color hues are of fundamental importance. According to various techniques of chromotherapy, the positive and strengthening effects of colors on psychophysical equilibrium can also be activated through foods.

To make a few simple examples, warm colors (such as red, orange and yellow) stimulate the appetite and re-awaken all the vital functions; cold colors (such as blue and purple), on the other hand, depress functions that are working in overdrive and hence, calm anxious and hyperactive individuals. Therefore, employing different chromatic ranges in dishes stimulates favorable action of the foods on the body, the mind and the mood.

Red is the color of love and of passion; it is a stimulating color that increases adrenalin contents in the blood, the heart and respiratory rates, and systemic blood pressure; it activates liver function, stimulates the central nervous system, courage, energy and vitality.

Pink is calming and relaxing; it expresses harmony and kindness, and is closely linked with the feminine and with fondness.

Orange transmits optimism and a desire to live. It stimulate growth, development, light-heartedness and wellbeing. It has an energizing, warming and cheering effect, in addition to expressing love.

Yellow is the symbol of light and strength; it is an antidepressant and improves the mood, learning, attention, concentration, communication and inter-personal relations.

Green creates equilibrium: it reduces hyper-stimulation produced by warm colors without loss of energy and attenuates the calming effect of cold colors while stimulating vigilance.

The variations of purple are pacifying and generate calm and serenity; they are great for anxious and easily excitable individuals.

Brown evokes ancient peasant traditions, the earth and wood, and transports one back to traditions and the mother's womb. It induces reflection and peace of mind.

White, on the other hand, is a symbol of openness, clarity and light. It expresses simplicity, innocence and purity.

Mixing two or more colors in foods can help equilibrate their specific characteristics, attenuating the stronger, more direct effects and adding a pinch of liveliness to the harmonious flow of unconscious and conscious information.

HEALTHY JUICES AND JUICES FOR LOSING WEIGHT

Today, weight-loss is one of the best solutions for staying healthy. Most of the diets available today work for the first month but lose their effect with time because most of the weight-loss is due to loss of water present in the body: as the water is lost, so is a lot of weight, but very little fat. This is why every low-calorie diet must be paired with physical exercise and water-rich foods, such as those foreseen by a liquid diet built around juices, centrifugal beverages and low-calorie smoothies.

Obviously the classic smoothies of cream, almonds and chocolate, or those with added sugar should be avoided and substituted with energizing, low-calorie and refreshing smoothies made from fresh fruit and vegetables, which are particularly helpful in the hot season but also in colder climates, for the prevention of flus. Such healthy and hydrating preparations are also beneficial to overall health. It is sufficient to combine, in an informed manner, low-calorie ingredients that will fill you up - cucumber, celery, raspberries, melon, cabbage, pomegranate, apple, pear and so on - and add spicy and aromatic components that can stimulate the metabolism and promote weight loss, such as ginger, pepper and chili pepper, or less exotic ingredients such as mint and lemon.

Consistency and eventual visits to medical specialists are essential.

FRUIT JUICES, EMULSIONS AND SMOOTHIES

EASY AND DELICIOUS

by Cinzia Trenchi

Smoothies are very easy to prepare, but certain fruit – such as apples, pears and melons with a hard and dense flesh – must be mixed with a liquid; if the season does not permit the use of ice, they should be mixed with juices. Citrus fruit rule this category: the lemon is a perfect accompaniment to any ingredient, but the mildly bitter grapefruit, the mandarin orange, with its embracing sweetness, and the orange, so beneficial that one forgets how delicious it is, are also excellent. Any type of fruit can be used to make smoothies, just let yourself be guided by the seasons and choose fruit that are at peak maturity, cut them into pieces, and remove the seeds and hard sections. The skin should only be used if the fruit is organic; and always remember that an organic fruit or vegetable is almost never perfect, smooth and defect-free! The same is true for juices prepared with the centrifugal juicer: be careful of skin in general and citrus fruit peel, which must be used in small doses and pieces, in particular. Every month of the year gifts us delicious fruit: you can choose among ripe strawberries, pineapple, raspberries, persimmons, blackberries, prickly pear and so on. You will be pleasantly surprised to discover that smoothies and juices prepared with ripe, naturally sweet fruit are so well-balanced, thirst-quenching and satisfying that preparing them will become a pleasant ritual. You will learn that juices and smoothies can be served as an aperitif, an end to a meal, a breakfast or an after workout snack. Discovering that a large glass of a delicious fruit beverage can equal a pair of cookies in its calorie content while being a lot more filling, will be a welcome surprise! However, you should be careful when choosing the fruit for use in juices: it is best not to use fruit with a low water content or a creamy consistency such as bananas and persimmons, for example.

VITAMINS AND ENERGY

by Maurizio Cusani

Fresh, seasonal fruit provide a healthy and quick-to-use energy source and guarantee a supply of the most important vitamins for maintaining our bodies healthy.

Wild berries, for example, contain extremely powerful antioxidants; citrus fruit are rich in vitamin C, while apples, pears and other woody fruit contain indigestible fiber, which is very useful to a healthy gastrointestinal system.

In our lives, there are many reasons for feeling in need of a quick energy boost. For example, we may happen to need a quick way to regain our calm after physical activity, training or an athletic competition: a dose of simple, rapid-absorption sugars contained in juices and smoothies accompanied by a significant amount of water is the ideal solution. Similarly, fruit juice concentrates can quickly supply strength to debilitated elderly individuals, children recovering from the flu, individuals returning from the hospital after surgery and to anyone who, for whatever reason, feels the need to regain a feeling of wellbeing in a short period.

Finally, juices and centrifuged beverages provide an extremely high supply of water to the body and are the obvious answer to all cases of dehydration, such as those that can occur in the summer, following gymnastic exercises and even those associated with gastrointestinal disorders.

2 servings   1 2/3 cups (300 g) fresh   2 oranges
                        pineapple

ORANGE AND PINEAPPLE SMOOTHIE

1. Remove the skin and the hard, fibrous portions of the pineapple. Cut it into pieces and transfer into the blender jar.

2. Peel the oranges and remove all of the white membrane covering the slices. Cut them into pieces and distribute over the pineapple.

3. Blend the ingredients until a homogeneous, smooth and fluid mixture is obtained.

4. Pour the smoothie into glasses and drink immediately.

5. The orange and pineapple smoothie is a perfect thirst-quencher. Suitable for the hot months, it can also be served with ice or diluted with a small amount of cold water.

Difficulty: EASY
Preparation: **10 minutes**
Calories: **94 kcal**
per serving

Recipe Properties:
The Orange and Pineapple Smoothie is a beverage that helps rehydrate the body and recover energy quickly, especially after bouts of the flu or illness in children. It is recommended in the summer and to help sustain the body during periods of stress or when debilitated by inflammatory diseases.

Orange *is rich in vitamins, particularly in vitamin C. It is a natural aid in the fight against winter illnesses. It contains calcium, zinc, copper and iron as well as numerous polyphenols with high antioxidant activity, and helps fight the signs of aging.*
Pineapple *can be used to treat swelling, cellulite, muscle trauma and circulatory problems. Bromelin, an enzyme contained in the fruit, also has an antiplatelet effect and renders blood more fluid. Pineapple pulp is a cure-all for those who have had thromboembolisms but it should be used in moderation when taking anticoagulation drugs.*

2 servings

1 banana
2 lemons

2/3 cup (100 g) currants
4 winter cherries

BANANA AND LEMON SMOOTHIE WITH WINTER CHERRIES AND CURRANTS

1. Peel the banana, cut into pieces and place into the blender.

2. Juice the lemons using a juicer and add to the bananas.

3. Wash the currant bunches and allow them to dry on a paper towel.

4. Open the calyx of the winter cherry plant but don't remove the fruit.

5. Blend the banana and the lemon juice until a homogeneous, soft cream is obtained then pour it into a glass. Decorate with the currant bunches and the winter cherries.

6. It is great as an original dessert or a quick breakfast.

Difficulty: EASY
Preparation: **10 minutes**
Calories: **110 kcal**
per serving

Recipe Properties:

The Banana and Lemon Smoothie with Winter Cherries and Currants is an energizing beverage that rehydrates and restores sugars after bursts of activity. In addition to its anti-oxidant properties, usefulness in the cold season and great taste, it is filling and a great for a weight-loss diet.

Winter cherry *is an exceptional source of vitamin C. According to Chinese medicine, it can help treat kidney stones. Its tannin content also makes it an excellent diuretic and depurative.*
Lemon *has the lowest sugar content of all the citrus fruit and is rich in fiber.*
Redcurrant, *together with blackcurrant, is one of the best known varieties of this fruit. It is characterized by great therapeutic properties. Already known for its antiaging properties, some studies have recently found it to have anti-tumor properties as well.*
Banana *is rich in natural carbohydrates such as glucose, fructose and sucrose, and boasts many characteristics that are beneficial to the body.*

PERSIMMON SMOOTHIE WITH MANDARIN ORANGE JUICE

1. Place the persimmon on a plate and remove the stem. Gently extract the pulp making sure to avoid the skin and transfer it to the blender jar.

2. Juice the mandarin oranges and pour the juice over the persimmon pulp.

3. Blend until a soft and smooth cream is obtained. Pour the mixture into a glass.

4. To enjoy this smoothie to the fullest, prepare it shortly before drinking. Persimmons oxidise quickly and can lose their freshness and flavor in just a few minutes!

5. A perfect energy boost with a great taste, this is one of the most filling smoothies. Therefore, it can be used to satisfy food cravings when on a weight-loss diet.

Difficulty: EASY
Preparation: **5 minutes**
Calories: **210 kcal**

Recipe Properties:

The Persimmon Smoothie with Mandarin Orange Juice is a highly energizing beverage that also has a high satiety index. Therefore, it is recommended for weight-loss diets.

It is great in cold climates and to fight winter illnesses.

Persimmon is a bright orange fruit, when mature, that originates in Japan and China. Its sweet pulp makes it very tasty even if sometimes, especially if the fruit is not fully ripe, it is slightly astringent due to the presence of tannins. IIn Japan, the juice of persimmons is used to cut and to clarify the national liquor: saké. Due to its high contents of potassium, sugars, beta-carotene and vitamin C, it is highly energizing and recommended for athletes, children and people facing a period of intense mental and physical stress.

Mandarin orange is rich in vitamin C and, in decreasing order, in vitamin A and B-group vitamins. In addition, it has high contents of fiber and minerals such as iron, magnesium and folic acid.

2 servings

2 lemons
11/2 cups (200 g) currants

1 cherimoya

CHERIMOYA, LEMON AND CURRANT SMOOTHIE

1. Wash and juice the lemons.

2. Wash the currant bunches. Carefully detach the berries and place them into the blender (set aside a tablespoon of berries for decorating the beverage if you wish).

3. Peel the cherimoya and remove the seeds. Cut the pulp and place over the currants.

4. Add the lemon juice and blend until a homogeneous and creamy mixture is obtained.

5. Fill the glasses and decorate as desired. Drink the smoothie immediately to enjoy the fresh fruit at their best.

Difficulty: EASY
Preparation: **10 minutes**
Calories: **85 kcal**
per serving

Recipe Properties:
The Cherimoya, Lemon and Currant Smoothie is a refreshing and thirst-quenching beverage that is great in any season and particularly great for preventing and curing winter illnesses. Its low calorie content makes it perfect for any weight-loss diet.

__Cherimoya__ is rich in vitamin C, minerals such as potassium and fiber, which is useful for people suffering from constipation. It has the same calorific value as the mango (75 calories per 100 grams of fruit). This fruit contains numerous polyphenol antioxidants called Annonaceous acetogenins that have a high antitumor activity. Since it is cytotoxic, it has also traditionally been used to fight intestinal parasites and worms.
__Lemon__ is astringent and, despite its high fiber contents, it is not recommended for people suffering from constipation.
__Currant__ is a berry, rich in anthocyanides and polyphenol antioxidants.

2 servings   10 1/2 oz. (300 g) ripe figs   1 organic orange

FIG AND ORANGE SMOOTHIE

1. Gently wash the figs. Remove the stem and the skin. Break into pieces and place into the blender jar.

2. Peel the oranges and set some of the peel aside for decorating the smoothie.

3. Remove the white portion of the orange. Cut the wedges and add them to the figs.

4. Blend the ingredients until a homogeneous mixture is obtained.

5. Pour the beverage into glasses, decorate with the orange peel set aside and serve immediately.

Difficulty: MEDIUM
Preparation: **10 minutes**
Calories: **95 kcal**
per serving

Recipe Properties:
The Fig and Orange Smoothie is the classic summer and fall remedy for people of all ages. A perfect energy boost after physical activity or during recovery after surgery or an illness. It is a stimulating and re-hydrating beverage that is quickly absorbed by the body.

***Fig** is rich in easily digestible sugars associated with minerals such as iron, calcium and phosphate.*
It is rich in vitamins A and C, as well as B-group vitamins, and has a good quantity of lignin (a plant fiber), which improves intestinal motility, making it ideal for people who suffer from constipation.
***Orange** can help you get your strength back during convalescence, a cold or after physical activity because of its vitamin contents. In addition, to vitamin C, it also contains vitamins of the B and P groups, citric acid and fiber, which help strengthen immune defenses.*

2 servings   10 1/2 oz. (300 g) ripe figs   1 lemon

FIG AND LEMON SMOOTHIE

1. Gently wash the figs. Remove the stem and some of the skin (leave about half on) then chop and transfer into the blender jar.

2. Juice the lemon. Filter the juice and pour over the figs.

3. Turn on the blender and blend until a soft and creamy mixture is obtained. Pour the smoothie into glasses and serve. It's a great dessert, magnificent breakfast or a snack that is full of virtues and benefits to the health. It should be drunk immediately in order to fully enjoy the natural sweetness of ripe figs lightly diluted by the flavor of the lemon.

Difficulty: MEDIUM
Preparation: **5 minutes**
Calories: **76 kcal**
per serving

Recipe Properties:

The Fig and Lemon Smoothie is an energizing beverage suitable for children as a snack or during convalescence. Even though it is low in calories, it has a high satiety index and is therefore recommended for weight-loss diets.

Fig *improves digestion and is a suitable addition to children's diets but is not recommended for people prone to colitis. It contains some mucilaginous substances useful for fighting different gastrointestinal disorders, such as dysphagia, gastritis, and peptic ulcers. Finally, this fruit is known for its diuretic and laxative properties.*

Lemon *can be of real help in the fight against winter respiratory illnesses. It contains vitamin C, A, many of the B-group vitamins and fiber.*

2 servings

2/3 cup (100 g) raspberries
2/3 cup (100 g) strawberries

1/4 cup (50 ml) raspberry juice

STRAWBERRY AND RASPBERRY SMOOTHIE WITH RASPBERRY JUICE

1. Gently wash the raspberries without submerging them in water then place them on a paper towel.

2. Remove the stems from the strawberries, place them into a strainer and wash under running water. Cut into pieces according to size and transfer into the blender jar.

3. Add the raspberries and the raspberry juice and turn on the blender. Blend until the smoothie is smooth and homogeneous.

4. If you prefer a beverage with none of the seeds found in strawberries and raspberries, use a centrifugal juicer instead of a blender.

Difficulty: EASY
Preparation: **5 minutes**
Calories: **80 kcal**
per serving

Recipe Properties:
The Strawberry and Raspberry Smoothie with Raspberry Juice sis an excellent beverage for individuals suffering metabolic disorders. In addition, it is detoxifying, low in calories and great for any weight-loss diet. It is a natural antidepressant, stimulant and mood regulator.

Strawberry *is characterized by a sponginess that facilitates the absorption of pesticides and preservatives. Consequently, it is important to use only organically cultivated berries..*
Raspberry *is a red, somewhat sour fruit that grows on bushes of the same name along forest edges and clearings. It is rich in vitamins C and A, citric acid, fructose, pectin, tannins, organic acids, ellagic acid and antioxidant flavonoids (polyphenols). Every one of these substances stimulates microcirculation and provides protection against tumor development.*

2 servings

1 lemon
2/3 cup (100 g) strawberries
2 bananas

2 wood toothpicks
5 ice cubes (optional)

STRAWBERRY, BANANA AND LEMON SMOOTHIE

1. Juice the lemon and filter the juice to eliminate any seeds.

2. Wash the strawberries under running water without submerging them. Remove the stems and set 2 strawberries aside for decorating the smoothie.

3. Peel the bananas and cut them into pieces. Dip two or three rounds into lemon juice to prevent browning and set aside for decorating.

4. Transfer the fruit into the blender jar, add the lemon juice and the ice if you want a more thirst-quenching smoothie.

5. Blend as long as necessary to obtain a smooth, soft cream.

6. Transfer into very cold glasses (place them into the freezer 10 minutes before use). Slide the set aside fruit onto the toothpicks and use them to decorate the smoothie. Drink this beverage, which is perfect for a refreshing, light breakfast or a low-fat but tasty dessert, immediately.

Difficulty: EASY
Preparation: **5 minutes**
Calories: **118 kcal**
per serving

Recipe Properties:

The Strawberry, Banana and Lemon Smoothie is thirst-quenching and stimulating. Useful for strengthening the body's defenses, it is filling and helps regulate moods and restore energy after intense activity or during convalescence.

Strawberry *contains vitamin C and folic acid, which is important to memory and during pregnancy. It is a low-calorie fruit that helps flush the body.*
Banana *is a very filling food that is rich in cholesterol-lowering substances, minerals, B-group vitamins and vitamins A and C.*
Lemon, *of possible Indian origins, is certainly one of the most famous citrus fruit of the Mediterranean. It is the fruit with the greatest amount of vitamin C: just 100 grams of the fresh fruit contains as much as 50 milligrams of vitamin C.*

2 servings   1 lb. (500 g) white melon   2 ripe kiwifruit

KIWIFRUIT SMOOTHIE WITH WHITE MELON JUICE

1. Clean the melon. Remove the seeds and the fibrous sections. Cut into pieces and extract the juice from 2/3 of the pulp in a centrifugal juicer.

2. Peel the kiwifruit, cut it into pieces and place into the blender jar together with the remaining melon. Add the melon juice and blend the ingredients until a homogeneous and creamy mixture is obtained.

3. Pour the smoothie into glasses and serve immediately in order to enjoy the sparkling freshness of these fruit rich in characteristics beneficial to a healthy diet at their best.

Difficulty: EASY
Preparation: **5 minutes**
Calories: **126 kcal**
per serving

Recipe Properties:

The Kiwifruit Smoothie with White Melon Juice is slimming, lightly laxative and a concentrate of antioxidants and rehydrating substances that fight aging and help prevent all cold season inflammatory illnesses. However, it should be consumed with caution by people suffering from springtime pollen allergies.

Kiwifruit helps regulate cholesterol due to its high content of antioxidants. It also facilitates circulation and slows down aging of the skin and the tissues of the eye. Similarly to plums and cooked vegetables, it is slightly laxative if consumed ripe. If consumed when not fully ripe, on the other hand, it is astringent.

White melon is a sweet, thirst-quenching fruit with water contents as high as 90%. Although it contains various sugars, it is extremely low in calories (just 33 calories per 100 grams) and is therefore an important part of a controlled weight-loss diet.

1 serving

1 lime
2 oz. (50 g) mango

2 passion fruit
1/4 cup (50 ml) coconut milk

MANGO, LIME AND PASSION FRUIT SMOOTHIE WITH COCONUT MILK

1. Juice the lime and pour the juice into a cup.

2. Peel the mango, cut it into pieces and transfer into the blender. Add the lime juice.

3. Cut the passion fruit into halves, remove the pulp using a spoon and add to the other ingredients. Finally, pour the coconut milk on top.

4. Blend all of the ingredients until a homogeneous beverage is obtained. Pour it into a glass and drink immediately.

5. With its rich, mouthwatering flavor and inviting aroma, this smoothie is a great source of energy to start your day.

Difficulty: EASY
Preparation: **3 minutes**
Calories: **230 kcal**

Recipe Properties:

The Mango, Lime and Passion Fruit Smoothie with Coconut Milk is rich and full of energizing nutrients. It is great for quickly recovering your strength and rehydrating after excessive physical activity, quenching your thirst and cooling down. It also has a high satiety index.

Passion fruit has a sweetish acidic taste that is somewhat sour. Originating in Brazil, this fruit is rich in vitamin C, potassium, fiber and beta-carotene. In addition, it contains a good quantity of Omega 6 fatty acids, which are good for the heart and circulation. It has anti-inflammatory and antioxidant properties.
Coconut milk has mild laxative and aphrodisiac effects.
Mango is a low-calorie fruit, which is very filling.
Lime is a great antiseptic for the oral cavity and protects the gums from inflammation.

2 servings

4 kiwifruit for the smoothie
and 1 for decorating
2 organic lemons

2 organic apples
leaves and flowers for decorating

APPLE AND KIWIFRUIT SMOOTHIE WITH LEMON JUICE

1. Wash the fruit. Peel the 4 kiwifruit and cut them into pieces.

2. Juice the lemons and grate 1 teaspoon lemon zest if you like its flavor.

3. Dice the apples and transfer all of the fruit into the blender. Add the lemon juice and zest, and blend until a uniform, creamy mixture is obtained.

4. Pour the beverage into glasses, add a few slices of the remaining kiwifruit and decorate with leaves and flowers. Serve immediately to enjoy the smoothie at its best.

Difficulty: EASY
Preparation: **5 minutes**
Calories: **110 kcal**
per serving

5. Excellent for breakfast or as a quick snack, and perfect as an aperitif.

Recipe Properties:

The Apple and Kiwifruit Smoothie with Lemon Juice is a refreshing snack that is light, low in calories, and rich in vitamins and minerals. Highly thirst-quenching and easily digestible, it is recommended for any time of the year.

Lemon juice, *in addition to its high content of beneficial substances, is highly thirst-quenching, great at binding the various flavors in smoothies and an excellent tool for preventing oxidation of the ingredients. If its flavor is liked, it should be included it in the daily diet.*
Kiwifruit *is very rich in vitamin C, retinol, folic acid and minerals.*
Apple *is composed of 85% water and has a detoxifying action on the body. It contains vitamins, minerals, organic acids and above all, pectin (primarily in the skin), which facilitate digestion and intestinal muscle contractions.*

2 servings

2 grapefruit
1 persimmon

1 ripe pear

PEAR SMOOTHIE WITH PERSIMMON AND GRAPEFRUIT JUICE

1. Juice a grapefruit and pour the juice into the blender jar.

2. Place a washed persimmon on a plate and remove the stem. Gently extract the pulp using a spoon making sure to avoid the skin. Add to the grapefruit juice.

3. Wash the other grapefruit and cut it into two halves. Using a sharp knife, extract the pulp (making sure not to cut through the peel) leaving behind two bowl-like containers. Add the pulp to the other ingredients.

4. Wash and peel the pear. Cut it into pieces and transfer into the blender.

5. Turn on the blender and let it run for the time required to obtain a fluid clump-free mixture. Fill the grapefruit containers with the smoothie and serve immediately.

Difficulty: MEDIUM
Preparation: **10 minutes**
Calories: **125 kcal**
per serving

Recipe Properties:

The Pear Smoothie with Persimmon and Grapefruit Juice is great for the elderly. It is depurative and hydrating, ans supplies a boost of energy to children and adults, who need to quickly replenish their mental and physical energy stores. It is very filling.

Persimmon *is energizing and perfect for athletes, children and adolescents, particularly if they need to improve their memorization and studying skills, or are about to engage in intense physical activity.*
Grapefruit *is a low-calorie fruit composed mostly of water. It contains pectin, vitamins A, C and E, bitter substances that strengthen the stomach and the lungs, and has a depurative action on the liver and kidneys. It has been recognized as a food that helps fight degenerative disorders.*
Pear *is rich in fiber, low in calories and has high water contents. It helps protect against osteoporosis and regularize intestinal transit.*

2 organic lemons
1 ripe pear

5 ice cubes (optional)

PEAR AND LEMON SMOOTHIE

1. Wash the lemons, grate 1 teaspoon full of lemon zest and tip it into the blender jar.

2. Peel the pear, cut it into pieces and add it to the lemon zest.

3. Juice the lemons and add the lemon juice to the other ingredients.

4. This smoothie is highly thirst-quenching and an excellent beverage for reintroducing liquids into the body after intense physical activity. If desired, add some ice and blend until a homogeneous mixture is obtained.

Difficulty: EASY
Preparation: **10 minutes**
Calories: **78 kcal**
per serving

Recipe Properties:

The Pear and Lemon Smoothie is reinvigorating, hydrating, filling and low in calories. It is recommended for people suffering from osteoporosis and hypertension. It is also very helpful for fighting the effects of old age in the elderly.

Pear *contains many simple sugars, such as fructose. It has a high satiety index and is rich in fiber, an element that makes it a good ally in weight-loss diets. Being easily digestible, it helps regulate movement through the intestine. By slowing down the fructose absorption rate, the fiber it contains helps maintain a constant level of energy during periods of heavy work and keeps the body hydrated.*

Lemon *is rich in a substance called limonene, which has been used successfully to treat gall bladder stones. According to recent American studies, its regular consumption may help prevent tumor formation.*

2 servings

2 organic apples
1 banana

1 organic pear

PEAR AND BANANA SMOOTHIE WITH APPLE JUICE

1. Wash the apples, cut them into pieces and place them into a centrifugal juicer obtaining freshly squeezed juice. If you are sure about the origins of the fruit, use the skin as well. If you are not, it is best to remove it.

2. Peel the banana and cut it into pieces making them fall directly into a blender.

3. Wash the pear, and only remove the core and seeds. Leave the skin, which is rich in fiber, on.

4. Add the apple juice to the chopped banana and blend for about 20 seconds or until the mixture is smooth and creamy.

5. Distribute the beverage among glasses and drink immediately.

Difficulty: EASY
Preparation: **10 minutes**
Calories: **130 kcal**
per serving

Recipe Properties:

The Pear and Banana Smoothie with Apple Juice is a rich, stimulating beverage suitable for constipation sufferers. Depurative and reinvigorating, it is ideal for weight-loss diets because it is incredibly filling. Great for osteoporosis, hypertension and age-related degeneration.

Apple is rich in pectin, which is a fiber that is very useful for the proper function of the gastrointestinal tract and can reduce glycemia.
Pear, with its high potassium contents, is perfect for low-sodium diets and hence, for hypertension sufferers. Also rich in elements such as boron and magnesium, it helps bind the calcium in bones and can prevent or slow down osteoporosis.
Banana contains many natural carbohydrates, a lot of fiber and minerals such as potassium and magnesium, in addition to amino acids such as tryptophan, which are very important for the nervous system.

2/3 cup (100 g) blueberries
10 strawberries

1 ripe and juicy pear
1 organic lemon

BLUEBERRY, STRAWBERRY AND PEAR SMOOTHIE

1. Wash the blueberries and the strawberries under running water without submerging them. Lay them out to drain on paper towels.

2. Remove the stems from the strawberries and cut each one into 2 to 4 pieces depending on the size of the fruit.

3. Wash the pear, peel it, and cut into pieces dropping them directly into the blender jar so that none of the juice is lost.

4. Grate 1 teaspoon of lemon zest and set aside. Juice the lemon. Filter the juice and pour it over the pear. Add the blueberries, strawberries and raspberries, and blend at low speed until a soft and creamy mixture is obtained.

5. Pour into a glass; add the lemon zest and mix. Drink right away to benefit fully from this surprisingly refreshing blend! If you want a smoothie that is not so dense, dilute it with half a glass of water.

Difficulty: EASY
Preparation: **10 minutes**
Calories: **90 kcal**

Recipe Properties:

The Blueberry, Strawberry and Pear Smoothie is low in calories, thirst-quenching and suitable for all weight-loss diets. Excellent for individuals wishing to improve their sight, and for those suffering from micro-circulatory or eye disorders.

Blueberry is a wild berry known for its beneficial effects on eyesight. In fact, it can improve night vision, particularly in near-sighted individuals, and has been proven to fight age-related oxidation of the macula, the most important portion of the retina.

Pear is a fruit (botanically speaking, a false fruit) of a tree of the same name. It is rich in antioxidants, particularly those of the polyphenol family, in vitamin C and in excellent fiber. It is great for prevention of cardiovascular diseases.

1 serving

2 prickly pears
1 small organic pear

Difficulty: MEDIUM
Preparation: **5 minutes**
Calories: **150 kcal**

PRICKLY PEAR AND PEAR JUICE

1. Before using prickly pears, it is best to equip yourself with gloves.

2. Wash the prickly pears in running water rubbing them for at least 1 minute then cut off the ends, incise the skin and roll it off. Place the pulp into a centrifugal juicer and catch the juice.

3. Wash the pear and if you are sure about its origins, juice it with the skin on.

4. Pour the juice into a stem glass. The liquid will appear opaque because the portion consisting of the foam and fiber tends to float to the surface. If you prefer a transparent juice, filter it through a strainer.

5. If you prefer a transparent juice, filter it through a strainer.

Prickly pear is very helpful in the fight against prostatic hyperplasia. It has high contents of fiber, which grant it laxative properties, and antioxidants such as betanin and indicaxanthin, which help combat cholesterol. It is not recommended for people suffering from diverticulosis because the high quantity of seeds may result in the formation of indigestible boluses.

Pear is rich in fiber, vitamin C and antioxidants, particularly those of the polyphenol family, which are a valid ally in the prevention of cardiovascular disease.

Recipe Properties:
The Prickly Pear and Pear Juice helps prevent cold season illnesses and regularize intestinal transit. It is great for people suffering from constipation and those who love exercising outdoors. It can contribute to winter and fall weight loss.

48

1 serving

11/2 cups (200 g)
  strawberries
1 organic orange
1 wood skewer
ice (optional)

Difficulty: EASY
Preparation: **8 minutes**
Calories: **88 kcal**

STRAWBERRY AND ORANGE JUICE

1. Wash the strawberries under running water without submerging them. Remove the stems and set aside 2 berries to use for the skewer.

2. Wash the orange, divide it into halves and cut away one wedge to use for decoration.

3. Juice the strawberries and then the orange in a centrifugal juicer. If you like the flavor of orange zest, use the fruit without peeling it; if not, remove the peel.

4. Pour the juice into a glass. Prepare a skewer with the strawberries and the orange slice, and add it to the juice.

5. The beverage is very thirst-quenching and with the addition of a few ice cubes, perfect for the summer months.

Strawberry whitens teeth and has anti-wrinkle and anti-cellulite properties. It contains a large amount of flavonoids (catechin, quercetin, kaempferol and anthocyanin), poly-phenols, resveratrol, vitamin C and ellagic acid: all of which are antioxidants.
Orange is rich in vitamins, above all in vitamin C and those of the B-group, and quickly restores any mineral loss, particularly potassium and magnesium. It is highly useful during the cold season and for flu prevention.

Recipe Properties:
The Strawberry and Orange Juice is a refreshing beverage excellent for children, athletes, flue sufferers and those following a weight-loss diet. Its visual appearance is pleasing; it is a mild stimulant.

2 servings

1 lemon
1 piece of ginger about 2 in. (5 cm) long

2 pomegranates
10 ice cubes

POMEGRANATE AND GINGER JUICE

1. Juice the lemon and filter the juice.

2. Peel the ginger and cut it into pieces. Wash the pomegranates and open them. Remove the white membrane from around the seeds. Tease the seeds out into a bowl and juice in a centrifugal juicer with the ginger.

3. Pour the pomegranate and ginger juice and the lemon juice into a cocktail shaker. Add the ice, mix and shake. Divide the beverage among glasses and serve.

4. Captivating in color and marvelously refreshing, this beverage is very thirst-quenching. It is perfect after physical activity, especially because ginger and lemon slow down the process of oxidation.

Difficulty: MEDIUM
Preparation: **15 minutes**
Calories: **770 kcal**
per serving

Recipe Properties:

The Pomegranate and Ginger Juice is a refreshing and reinvigorating beverage with an intense aroma. It is a recommended addition to weight-loss diets; it provides an excellent supply of antioxidants and compounds that actively combat inflammatory and cold season illnesses.

Pomegranate *is a fruit rich in vitamin C and important compounds such as the flavonoids, which stimulate the immune system and have a positive effect on bone health, heart, blood vessels and endocrine glands. Its consumption promotes increasing urine production and contrasts mood swings typical of menopause. Finally, the fiber it contains helps digestion.*

Ginger *has a considerable detoxifying action, greatly aids digestion and stimulates gall bladder function. It has anti-inflammatory properties and helps relieve nausea caused by seasickness, airsickness and pregnancy.*

1 serving

1 organic pink grapefruit
1 organic lemon

4 cardamom pods
1 pinch of cinnamon

SPICED GRAPEFRUIT AND LEMON JUICE

1. This juice is very quick and easy to prepare! Just use a lemon juicer or a centrifugal juicer being careful to completely remove the white membrane covering the lemon and grapefruit wedges and to use a small amount of rind (only if the fruit is organic!) cut into small pieces.

2. Crush the cardamom pods in a mortar. Wash the citrus fruit and cut them into halves. Set aside a slice of the lemon for decorating the juice. Juice the fruit in a lemon juicer or a centrifugal juicer.

3. Pour the juice into a glass, add the crushed cardamom, decorate with the slice of lemon and sprinkle with the cinnamon.

4. Drink this juice immediately to fully enjoy its surprisingly good flavor and unique properties.

Difficulty: EASY
Preparation: **10 minutes**
Calories: **50 kcal**

Recipe Properties:
The Spiced Grapefruit and Lemon Juice is very reinvigorating, hydrating and refreshing. It is a beverage that helps strengthen immune defenses and combat cold season and dehydration related illnesses. Its consumption is recommended for diets and for slowing aging.

Lemon combats age-related disorders and capillary fragility.
Grapefruit is rich in vitamin C and can improve blood vessel health and circulation. It has anti-flu, anti-inflammatory and regenerative properties and improves immune defenses. It slows aging, oxygenates tissues and combats cellulite.
Cardamom is considered a "fat burning" spice because it stimulates the metabolism. It has digestion-aiding and anti-inflammatory properties and strengthens the immune system.
Cinnamon is helpful during convalescence, and is anti-inflammatory and digestive. It has a positive action on mood and seems to have an aphrodisiac effect as well.

2 servings

2/3 cup (100 g) currants   11/2 cups (200 g) strawberries
11/2 cups (200 g) raspberries   1/4 cup (50 ml) mineral water

FILTERED STRAWBERRY, RASPBERRY AND CURRANT JUICE

1. Separately, clean the strawberries, raspberries and currants. Set aside some berries for decoration.

2. Detach the current berries from the stems and gently crush them in a mortar (marble, if possible) then pass through a strainer and catch the juice in a container.

3. Separately, repeat the same procedure for the raspberries and the strawberries. This procedure, which is rather long, will guarantee an excellent result!

4. Finally, mix the current, raspberry and strawberry juices, dilute with a small amount of water and pour into glasses.

5. Decorate with the remaining fruit and serve immediately.

Difficulty: MEDIUM
Preparation: **20 minutes**
Calories: **70 kcal**
per serving

Recipe Properties:
The Filtered Strawberry, Raspberry and Currant Juice is a beverage that helps protect against all age-related diseases. Specifically, it is rich in active substances beneficial to circulation, has anti-tumor properties and stimulates the central nervous system.

__Strawberry__ is composed of 90% water and contains a considerable quantity of antioxidants. It is useful in weight-loss diets, rehydration and to combat cellulite.
__Raspberry__ is rich in vitamins (above all C and A), citric acid, fructose, pectin and tannins, but above all, in a very powerful antioxidant flavonoid.
__Redcurrant__ has considerable quantities of antioxidants, above all flavonoids, which combat degenerative diseases. It also has anti-inflammatory and anti-viral properties.

VEGETABLE JUICES, EMULSIONS AND SMOOTHIES

NUTRITIOUS AND FLAVORFUL

by Cinzia Trenchi

"They are not sweet" is the key phrase of this section dedicated mainly to vegetables: bitter, spicy and aromatic ingredients are all welcome! Vegetables can transform themselves into exquisite juices, thirst-quenching smoothies, and appetizing and nutritious emulsions with unexpected flavor nuances and intriguing combinations of color and taste.

With their high water contents, vegetables are an excellent ingredient for juices that boast excellent properties extremely useful in a low-calorie diets while being every bit as great in their beauty and richness of flavor as a sumptuous plate of mixed vegetables.

Almost all vegetables lend themselves to the preparation of juices: the dark green and mildly bitter extract of the marvelous chicory can be attenuated with soybean sprouts; other excellent ingredients include spinach, broccoli, fennel, carrots, celeriac and many more.

You will be surprised by the colors that the preparations will take on: the intense red of the beet, charged orange of the carrot and many shades of green, from the lighter shades of celery to the richer shades of broccoli. The deep purple of black cabbage and clear greens, yellows and reds of bell peppers. A light and soft foam and an almost imperceptible suspension of particles complete these preparations, which are as beautiful as they are healthy. Sometimes, the addition of a small amount of citrus juice is more of a condiment than a bona fide ingredient: in fact, just a few drops of lemon, lime or orange juice are sufficient to dampen an intense flavor that may prove difficult to appreciate at first tasting. Not to mention the emulsions, which thanks to a few drops of oil gift us with softness and an airy creaminess: this is the case of tomato, cucumber and celeriac emulsions. Aromatic herbs and spices are always welcome to add aroma, flavor and a special touch to such a simple and delicious preparation.

VITAL ANTIOXIDANTS

by Maurizio Cusani

Fundamental to our health and true protagonists of our wellbeing, vegetables are an irreplaceable source of vitamins, minerals and fiber. Their color is a sign of the presence of certain active ingredients: those with a yellow-orange color (such as carrot and pumpkin), for example, are rich in vitamin A and carotenoids; those with a green color (such as spinach and lettuce) are rich in lutein and folates; and those red in color (such as tomatoes and bell peppers) are rich in lycopenes and antioxidants. This is why choosing vegetables that are varied in color is the correct strategy for disease prevention. In addition, it will ensure a result that is pleasant to the eye and stimulating to the nervous system.

Vegetable-based beverages are low in calories, ensure a high satiety index and are extremely rich in antioxidants that are vital for maintaining our bodies young. Therefore, vegetable smoothies and juice concentrates are excellent for losing weight and for staying young and active. Inevitably, however, these beverages are less energizing with respect to those of fruit and the energy surge is not immediate. Nevertheless, often, they have actions on our organs that are more selective.

For the liver, for example, bitter herbs and other wild greens such as dandelion, are very useful, but so are beets, carrots and celery mixed with herbs such as oregano, mint and others. Cruciferous vegetables (black cabbage, broccoli and the like), well known for their antioxidant, anti-aging and anti-tumor properties, combat degenerative diseases, especially if consumed raw.

In addition, it should be kept in mind that the fibrous portion of the vegetables slows down the absorption of sugars by the gastrointestinal tract; this is beneficial to the pancreas, which is not shocked into a sudden frenzy of insulin production. Therefore, individuals prone to diabetes should give preference to vegetable smoothies over those made with fruit.

1 serving

6 cherry tomatoes
6 asparagus
1/2 cup (100 ml) vegetable broth

1 tsp. extra virgin olive oil
salt and pepper

ASPARAGUS AND TOMATO SMOOTHIE

1. Wash the tomatoes. Cut them into pieces and place in a blender with half a teaspoon of oil, salt, pepper and 2 tablespoons of broth if desired.

2. Blend until a soft and smooth emulsion is obtained. Pour into a glass and was the blender jar.

3. Wash the asparagus, remove the hard, woody portions and chop. Place into the blender with room-temperature vegetable broth, remaining oil, 1 pinch of salt and pepper to taste.

4. Pour the asparagus smoothie on top of the tomato cream and drink immediately. This light but great-tasting preparation can be an excellent substitute for a first course.

Difficulty: EASY
Preparation: **10 minutes**
Calories: **120 kcal**

Recipe Properties:
The Asparagus and Tomato Smoothie is highly diuretic and depurative. It has anti-inflammatory and weight-loss properties. It contains sulfur-rich compounds that reduce arterial pressure and can improve the working of the heart.

Tomato, *thanks to its lycopene content, is a valid aid against water retention and for maintaining a good skin tone.*
Asparagus *belongs to the same botanical family as garlic and aloe: plants that contain many sulfured compounds with anti-inflammatory, hypotensive, cardiotonic, expectorant, anti-parasitic and anti-diabetic actions. It is rich in saponins, polyphenols and potassium: elements that render the vegetable highly diuretic. Hence, it is traditionally used to flush out the kidneys, the bronchioles and the liver. Its high water content ensures a high satiety index and a low calorie content, which makes it ideal for weight-loss diets.*

2 servings

7 oz. (200 g) celery
2 carrots

2 oranges
salt and pepper

CARROT, CELERY AND ORANGE SMOOTHIE

1. Wash the celery and remove any damaged portions. Cut it into pieces small enough for the centrifugal juicer and extract the juice.

2. Wash the carrots. Peel or grate them, as you prefer, and cut into pieces small enough to be blended well.

3. Cut the oranges into halves and juice them. If you like the flavor of orange zest and if the fruit are organic, you can add small pieces of the peel to the other ingredients in the blender or the centrifugal juicer.

4. Since the zest has a very strong flavor and can overwhelm the flavor of the other ingredients, we suggest using small amounts, unless you are used to this flavor.

5. Blend the carrots with the orange and the celery juices. Stir, season with salt and pepper to taste, and enjoy this reinvigorating and vitamin-rich concoction as soon as possible.

Difficulty: EASY
Preparation: **10 minutes**
Calories: **140 kcal**
per serving

Recipe Properties:
The Carrot, Celery and Orange Smoothie is a beverage that is flushing, depurative, anti-inflammatory, low in calories and rich in antioxidants, which combat free radicals, substances that are responsible for all of the degenerative tissue and age-related diseases.

Celery is a depurative, diuretic, and a natural stimulant due to its content of aspartic acid.
Orange, which is rich in vitamin C, is depurative and anti-inflammatory. It is an excellent source of antioxidants, which reinforce the immune system and regularize the metabolism, in addition to combatting cellular aging provoked by free radicals. Finally, it has diuretic properties and is a valid ally against the formation of cellulite.
Carrot simprove twilight vision and are rich in vitamin A and B-group vitamins, minerals and fiber. Their sugars are rapidly digested.

2 servings

2 cucumbers
4 green onions
1 bunch of aromatic herbs:
    wild fennel, oregano, sage and
    borage

2 limes
1 tbsp. extra virgin olive oil
salt and pepper
edible flowers for decoration

CUCUMBER SMOOTHIE WITH LIME JUICE, GREEN ONIONS AND AROMATIC HERBS

1. Wash the cucumbers, the green onions and the herbs. Juice the lime and filter the resulting juice. Remove half of the skin from the cucumbers, trim the ends and cut into small pieces. (This makes blending with a small amount of liquids easier!)

2. Remove the external layers from the green onions, cut off the roots and dark green leaves. Cut into pieces and combine with the cucumber. Add 1 sage leaf, 1 pinch of wild fennel and oregano, and 2 borage leaves then pour the mixture into the blender jar.

3. Add the lime juice, oil, salt and pepper to taste, and blend for the time necessary to obtain a soft and smooth consistency.

4. Divide the smoothie among glasses, decorate with the left over herbs and flowers, and serve immediately.

5. This smoothie is an excellent cold first course perfect for supplying a store of low-calorie, great tasting health benefits during the hot months!

Difficulty: EASY
Preparation: **8 minutes**
Calories: **90 kcal**
per serving

Recipe Properties:

The Cucumber Smoothie with Lime Juice, Green Onions and Aromatic Herbs is a healthy beverage great for weight-loss and detoxifying diets due to its low-calorie content and high satiety index. Its high antioxidant content makes it important for the prevention of all age-related diseases.

Cucumber, originating in northern India, has been cultivated in southern Europe for millennia. It is ideal for low-calorie diets because it is rich in tartaric acid, which impedes the transformation of sugars into fats and has a high satiety index.

Green onion, like the onion, is a very flavorful and aromatic bulb that is rich in minerals and vitamins.

Lime contains compounds that fight rheumatism and autoimmune diseases.

Aromatic herbs (thyme, oregano, sage, etc.) are rich in antioxidants and flavonoids.

2 servings

1 celery heart
2 carrots
8 leaves of purple sage

1/2 cup (50 g) pre-cooked corn
salt and pepper

CORN SMOOTHIE WITH CARROT AND CELERY JUICE

1. Clean the celery, wash it and cut into pieces small enough for the centrifugal juicer.

2. Trim the ends of the carrots. Peel or grate them, as you prefer, then dice and add to the celery.

3. Wash the sage; dry it and set aside.

4. Transfer the carrots and celery into the centrifugal juicer. Catch the juice and pour it into the blender jar.

5. Add the corn and run the blender until a soft, smooth and evenly mixed cream is obtained.

6. Season with salt and pepper to taste, decorate with sage leaves and serve immediately.

7. Perfect as a substitute for a first course or as a snack, this smoothie is an extremely pleasant and satisfying beverage that will fill you up.

Difficulty: EASY
Preparation: **10 minutes**
Calories: **140 kcal**
per serving

Recipe Properties:
The Corn Smoothie with Carrot and Celery Juice is eubiotic and beneficial for the digestive system as a whole, in addition to being low in calories and conducive to weight loss. It purifies the body, particularly the liver and kidneys. Hence, it is an excellent detoxifier, diuretic and decongestant.

Corn or maize, is a grain of the Poaceae family. In addition to unsaturated fats and minerals (potassium, magnesium, selenium, zinc and copper), it contains vitamins A and E as well as the B-group vitamins, and has high contents of biological amino acids, fiber and above all, starch, which composes 80-85% of the kernel.
Carrot juice is great for stabilizing intestinal flora and ideal during bouts of the stomach flu or after taking antibiotics.
Celery has a depurative and diuretic effect on the body.

2 servings

2 bell peppers
2/3 cup (100 g) cherry
  tomatoes
1 green onion
2 limes
5 ice cubes
salt and pepper

Difficulty: EASY
Preparation: **10 minutes**
Calories: **53 kcal**
per serving

BELL PEPPER, GREEN ONION AND LIME SMOOTHIE

1. Wash the bell peppers. Remove the stems, seeds and white portions, and cut into pieces. Wash the cherry tomatoes. Remove the stems, and cut into 2 or 4 parts, depending on their size.

2. Wash the green onion. Remove the external layers, the dark green portions and the roots. Cut it into pieces and set a little bit aside to use to add extra flavor and decorate the smoothie.

3. Juice the lime using a juicer. Pour the juice into the blender jar; add the green onion, cherry tomatoes, bell pepper and ice. Blend all the ingredients until a smooth and homogeneous mixture is obtained.

4. Season with salt and pepper, divide among glasses, decorate with pieces of green onion and serve immediately. This smoothie is perfect for the hot months. It is refreshing, appetizing and makes a wonderful aperitif.

Recipe Properties:
The Bell Pepper, Green Onion and Lime Smoothie is suitable for any weight-loss treatment. Its ingredients burn fats and have depurative and antioxidants properties. It is an excellent beverage for regaining energy, above all for adults and the elderly.

Lime contains an abundance of citric acid, which dissolves fats and hence, helps lose weight.
Green onion is expectorant and diuretic. It reinvigorates the digestive system and reduces blood sugar levels.
Pepper is rich in carotenoids and antioxidants.

2 servings

3 tomatoes
2 green onions
10 olives
10 salt-preserved
  capers
1 tbsp. extra virgin
  olive oil

Difficulty: EASY
Preparation: **10 minutes**
Calories: **110 kcal**
per serving

TOMATO, OLIVE, GREEN ONION AND CAPER SMOOTHIE

1. Wash and peel the tomatoes. Remove the seeds and break into pieces, letting them fall directly into the blender jar.

2. Wash the green onions, remove the external layers, cut off the roots and dark green leaves (set aside two leaves to use for decoration) then cut into small pieces.

3. Add the green onions, 2 or 3 olives, 4 capers (without rinsing them in water) and oil to a blender and blend for the time necessary to obtain a soft and smooth cream.

4. Pour the mixture into glasses, decorate with pieces of green onion leaves and accompany with the remaining olives and capers.

Tomato greately stimulates the metabolism and combats stretch marks.
Caper is a discreet source of proteins, vitamins A, E and K, B-group vitamins, and minerals such as iron, copper, manganese and magnesium.
Olive is rich in oleic acid, which protects the circulation. It contains fat-soluble vitamins and phytosterols with substantial antioxidant and anti-ageing properties.
Green onion has a considerable nutritional value thanks to its mineral and vitamin C contents.

Recipe Properties:
The Tomato, Olive, Green Onion and Caper Smoothie is tasty and low in calories. It is rich in nutrients: unsaturated fatty acids, vitamins and above all in minerals. It is stimulating and facilitates digestion.

67

2 servings

2 cups (300 g) well ripe cherry tomatoes
1 bunch of sage, basil and oregano

2 tbsp. extra virgin olive oil
2 tbsp. lemon juice
salt and pepper

TOMATO SMOOTHIE WITH FRESH OREGANO

1. Wash the tomatoes, cut them in 2 or 4 pieces depending on their size and transfer into a blender.

2. Clean the aromatic herbs. Set some leaves aside to use for decoration and add the rest to the tomato.

3. Add the oil, 2 oregano tips, the lemon juice, and salt and pepper to taste.

4. You can prepare this emulsion using either a tabletop or an immersion blender.

5. Blend the ingredients until a smooth, foamy and soft mixture is obtained.

6. Pour the mix into glasses and decorate with the remaining aromatic herbs, which render it more pleasant to the eye and even more pleasant to the taste.

7. Appetizing and rich in flavor and textures, it is an excellent appetizer or tasty snack for the summertime!

Difficulty: EASY
Preparation: **8 minutes**
Calories: **115 kcal**
per serving

Recipe Properties:

The Tomato Smoothie with Fresh Oregano is an anti-ageing beverage that is rich in antioxidants. Suitable for weight-loss diets and for prevention of cellulite formation and circulatory diseases. It has antiseptic properties and plays an important role in slowing down prostate aging.

__Tomato__ is a very important source of antioxidants because it contains vitamins A and E, lycopene and beta-carotene. All of these substances are known for their anti-tumor and anti-degenerative properties. They are beneficial to the heart and the circulation, and protect the eyesight. Lycopene is more active cooked than raw.

__Oregano__ is an aromatic herb that is rich in phenolic antioxidants, vitamins and minerals such as iron, potassium, calcium and manganese. It has fair anti-inflammatory, antiseptic and antibacterial properties beneficial above all during respiratory illnesses. It protects against prostate tumors. Of the vitamins, it contains, above all, vitamin C.

2 servings

1 celery heart
2 medium, ripe tomatoes
7 oz. (200 g) cleaned celeriac

1 tbsp. extra virgin olive oil
1/4 cup (50 ml) tomato juice
salt and pepper

CELERIAC AND TOMATO SMOOTHIE

1. Clean the celery heart. Keep a few leaves to use for decoration and cut the rest into pieces small enough for the blender.

2. Wash the tomatoes. Remove the stems and if you wish, the skin and the seeds.

3. Cut the celeriac into small pieces. Place them into the blender jar together with oil, celery, tomato juice and chopped tomato.

4. Blend until the soft and smooth cream is obtained. Season to taste, stir and pour into cups or stem glasses. Decorate with celery leaves and serve immediately.

Difficulty: EASY
Preparation: **10 minutes**
Calories: **50 kcal**
per serving

Recipe Properties:
The Celeriac and Tomato Smoothie is a slimming, flushing, depurative and low-calorie beverage rich in anti-tumor and anti-degenerative substances. It helps combat all circulatory and vascular diseases.

Tomato *is composed of over 90% water, some carbohydrates and almost no fats. Nearly 2% of a tomato is composed of fiber and about 1% of protein. The sugars include glucose and fructose, while the most abundant acids are citric acid, which represents 90% of total acids, and malic acid.*
Celeriac *is a vegetable that is extremely low in calories. Its flavor, which is slightly less intense than that of celery, makes it suitable for recipes in which it serves not just to add flavor, but as the main ingredient.*

2 servings   10 1/2 oz. (300 g) baked beet   7 oz. (200 g) celeriac
2 lemons

BEET, CELERIAC AND LEMON JUICE

1. Remove the external portion of the beet and cut into pieces.

2. Cut the celeriac into pieces small enough for the centrifugal juicer.

3. Juice the lemons and filter the juice.

4. Extract the juice from the celeriac and then the baked beet in a centrifugal juicer. Combine with the lemon juice, stir and pour into glasses.

5. It is an excellent aperitif with a captivating color and pleasant flavor, but above all, it is an excellent aid to weight loss because it favors the elimination of fats!

Difficulty: EASY
Preparation: **10 minutes**
Calories: **60 kcal**
per serving

Recipe Properties:
The Beet, Celeriac and Lemon Juice is not just slimming but also highly energizing and rich in compounds that help reestablish a psychophysical equilibrium. This beverage has a high satiety index and many substances that help protect the body.

Beet *is a low-calorie vegetable that contains a balanced proportion of proteins, fiber and sugars. It is rich in potassium and vitamins A and C. Because the nitrates it contains optimize oxygen consumption reducing physical strain and improving athletic performance, its extracts can also improve endurance.*
Lemon *keeps teeth, gums, and veins healthy and facilitates the healing of wounds.*
Celeriac *contains potassium, calcium, phosphate, magnesium, selenium and a good amount of vitamins A, C and K, in addition to fiber.*

1 serving

7 oz. (200 g) broccoli
1/2 cup (50 g) soybean sprouts

1 tsp. apple vinegar
salt and pepper (optional)

BROCCOLI AND SOYBEAN SPROUT JUICE

1. Wash the broccoli. Let it soak for a few minutes then drain and cut into pieces small enough for the centrifugal juicer.

2. Clean the sprouts. Rinse and let then drain in a colander.

3. Place the broccoli and 2/3 of the sprouts into a centrifugal juicer and catch the juice. Season it with vinegar and with salt and pepper to taste.

4. Pour the juice into a stem glass or a normal glass. Arrange the remaining sprouts on top and drink this healthy beverage immediately.

5. This mixture can also serve as an excellent dressing for soups, salads or tossed vegetables.

Difficulty: EASY
Preparation: **10 minutes**
Calories: **70 kcal**

Recipe Properties:
The Broccoli and Soybean Sprout Juice is not only slimming and detoxifying, but also rich in antioxidants that help prevent degenerative and vascular diseases, and cancer. This beverage is particularly suitable to adults and the elderly.

Broccoli, *like all cruciferous vegetables, has anti-tumor properties and due to its high lutein contents, helps preserve eyesight, particularly if eaten raw. It is low in calories, rich in fiber and a great addition to weight-loss and recovery diets.*
Soybean sprouts, *raw or cooked, have properties beneficial to our bodies. They are diuretic, and help lower cholesterol and clean the arteries. Hence, they are recommended for those who must follow a particularly healthy diet. The few calories contained in raw soybean sprouts make them perfect for low-calorie diets.*

2 servings

1 grapefruit
4 carrots
1 tbsp. extra virgin olive oil

1 tsp. spice mix: black and pink
pepper, cumin, dried aromatic
herbs
salt

CARROT AND GRAPEFRUIT JUICE WITH SPICES

1. Wash the grapefruit, cut it into halves and juice it. Catch the juice then filter it.

2. Wash the carrots and scrape or peel them, as you prefer. Cut them into pieces small enough for the masticating or centrifugal juicer.

3. Catch the resulting juice and combine it with the grapefruit juice.

4. Season with oil, aromatic herbs and spices freshly crushed in a mortar.

5. Add salt to taste and mix, then pour into glasses and drink immediately.

6. The beverage is recommended for those who love articulated, intriguing flavors. In addition to being extremely thirst-quenching, the richness of its flavor means that it can be used as a cold first course.

Difficulty: EASY
Preparation: **8 minutes**
Calories: **144 kcal**
per serving

Recipe Properties:

The Carrot and Grapefruit Juice with Spices is an energizing and healthy beverage suitable for weight-loss diets, as protection against all age-related degenerative diseases, and for prevention of circulatory and vascular diseases, and different cancers.

Grapefruit *contains pectin, and vitamins A, C and E. It has been recognized to have a beneficial action against degenerative diseases.*
Carrot, *the most consumed edible root, contains easily assimilated sugars, many minerals and fiber.*
Spices *(pepper, ginger, cinnamon, nutmeg, etc.) stimulate the metabolism, are low in calories and easy to digest.*
Extra virgin olive oil *(EVO) is rich in antioxidants beneficial to circulation and favors useful cholesterol by reducing the level of bad cholesterol in the body.*

1 serving   10 1/2 oz. (300 g) red cabbage   **1 fennel**

RED CABBAGE AND FENNEL JUICE

1. Clean the cabbage and fennel. Wash them and cut into pieces small enough for a centrifugal juicer.

2. Juice the cabbage and fennel together; fennel is a water-rich vegetable that can also facilitate the extraction of liquids from the red cabbage leaves.

3. Pour the juice into a glass, stir and drink immediately to fully enjoy the benefits of this beverage.

4. Red cabbage has a very intense color and if you prefer a lighter color to your juice, you can dilute with mineral water or ice. This beverage is of great help to our wellbeing thanks to its wide range of properties, which render it an important ally to our health.

Difficulty: EASY
Preparation: **10 minutes**
Calories: **45 kcal**

Recipe Properties:
The Red Cabbage and Fennel Juice is used in the nutraceutical field for its ability to prevent degenerative diseases resulting from oxidation by free radicals, particularly in women. It is perfect for weight-loss diets.

Red cabbage *is an ideal eubiotic for treating ulcerative colitis and gastric ulcers. It helps combat anemia by facilitating the production of red blood cells. It contains indole, sulphoraphane (a sulfur-based compound at the source of the unpleasant cabbage smell) and other antioxidants beneficial for the prevention of all age-related degenerative diseases.*
Fennel *is very rich in vitamins, above all in vitamin A, and minerals (potassium, calcium and phosphorus), all substances that are useful for athletic activity, and for maintenance and equilibrium of intestinal transit. It is also useful for combatting constipation and stomach gas.*

1 serving

1 head of any chicory
   variety (sugarloaf,
   Belgian endive)

1 cup (100 g) sprouts of soybeans
   or other seeds
1 tsp. apple vinegar
salt

CHICORY AND SPROUT (CRESS, SOYBEAN, FENNEL) JUICE

1. Carefully wash the salad. Do not remove the core and the roots, and reduce into pieces small enough for the juicer.

2. Clean the sprouts. Wash, drain and set some aside to use for decoration. Place the rest of the sprouts into the juicer first. Add the chicory and catch the juice into a glass.

3. This juice has a very intense color and refreshing taste that recalls the springtime.

4. If you use chicory that is very bitter, adding some apple vinegar will attenuate the taste of the beverage and 1 pinch of salt will complete it.

5. Drink this beverage immediately. This mixture is a true cure-all: it supplies a boost of minerals, quenches your thirst and even provides a mild detoxification of the body.

Difficulty: EASY
Preparation: **10 minutes**
Calories: **40 kcal**

Recipe Properties:
The Chicory and Sprout (Cress, Soybean, Fennel) Juice is low in calories and slimming. It contains many antioxidants, excellent depurative properties and protects emunctory organs and organs of detoxification.

Chicory *is an herbaceous plant that contains fiber, potassium, calcium, iron, a lot of vitamins C, P and K, and B-group vitamins. The bittery-tasting chicoric acid, which is present in large amounts, performs a depurative, diuretic and digestive action and protects the kidneys and liver. Therefore, chicory helps fight mild tympanites, constipation, irritable bowel and diabetes. The vegetable also contains derivatives of caffeic acid, which render chicory a poor choice for suffers of gastric or peptic ulcers and those taking beta-blocking drugs for heart problems or high blood pressure.*
Sprouts *(soybean, fennel or cress) are very rich in vitamins and antioxidants.*

1 serving   **2 fennels**   **4 de-salted capers**
                  5 almonds

FENNEL, CAPERS AND ALMOND JUICE

1. Wash the fennel. Remove the tops and cut into pieces small enough for the centrifugal juicer.

2. Finely crush the almonds in a mortar and mince the capers.

3. Juice the fennel in a centrifugal juicer. Catch the juice and add the almonds and capers.

4. Stir the beverage, pour it into a glass and drink immediately.

5. This juice is a concentrate of freshness and flavor recommended for instances of "lazy bowels". It is extremely balanced and has a pleasant flavor in which the sweetness of the almonds blends perfectly with the aroma of fennel and the Mediterranean flavor of the capers.

Difficulty: EASY
Preparation: **10 minutes**
Calories: **50 kcal**

Recipe Properties:

The Fennel, Capers and Almond Juice is low in calories and has a mildly diuretic and stimulating action. Suitable for all ages, it is rich in antioxidants that defend against free radicals, and great for getting your strength back after intense athletic activity.

__Caper__ is often preserved in salt and it is best to carefully desalt it by repeatedly soaking in water and squeezing it out, particularly if you have high blood pressure or cardiovascular disease. It stimulates the appetite, favors digestion and is diuretic.

__Almond__ is an oil-rich nut that can help normalize intestinal lumen and regulate cholesterol thanks to its high concentrations of unsaturated fats. It is rich in calories (542 per 100 grams) but also filling.

__Fennel__ improves digestion, and helps flush the body and reduce the amount of calories assumed from the almonds.

2 servings

1 fennel

7 oz. (200 g) Savoy cabbage heart

1 celery heart

FENNEL, CABBAGE AND CELERY JUICE

1. Clean all the vegetables. Wash them, set aside a few celery leaves, and cut into pieces small enough for a juicing press, a masticating juicer or a centrifugal juicer.

2. Extract the juice from the vegetables, stir and pour into glasses. Decorate the beverage with the remaining celery leaves.

3. In this juice, the dominant cabbage flavor (which is extremely important to our health but not always desirable!) is rendered more delicate by the light and aromatic flavor of fennel, producing a pleasantly thirst-quenching result.

Difficulty: EASY
Preparation: **10 minutes**
Calories: **40 kcal**
per serving

Recipe Properties:
The Fennel, Cabbage and Celery Juice, in addition to being low in calories and slimming, helps prevent age-related degenerative, cardiovascular, and sensory (skin, eyesight, hearing, etc.) diseases and cancer. It is a depurative and detoxifying beverage.

Fennel is an herbaceous plant common throughout the Mediterranean. Its peculiar aroma is due to significant concentrations of anethol. It is a fiber-rich vegetable.
Cabbage is a typical winter vegetable. The consumed parts of the vegetable include the green leaves and inflorescences (broccoli). It is very popular in diets because of it's vegetable protein and low calorie contents, high concentrations of vitamin C (double that of the same weight in oranges), vitamins A and K, B-group vitamins, and minerals such as potassium, copper, iron, calcium and phosphorus.
Celery has long been used as an aphrodisiac.

1 serving

1 cup (200 g) fresh spinach
2 lemons

1 tsp. sesame seeds
salt and pepper (optional)

SPINACH JUICE WITH LEMON AND SESAME SEEDS

1. Clean the spinach and let it soak in cold water until all the earth has detached from the leaves. Rinse without squeezing out excess water because residual water will not affect the flavor of the beverage!

2. Peel the lemons, eliminate the white portions and cut into pieces small enough for a centrifugal juicer or a juicing press.

3. Lightly toast, just a few seconds, the sesame seeds in a non-stick frying pan to render the fats in the seeds easier to assimilate.

4. In a centrifugal juicer, first juice the spinach, then the lemon in order to obtain a beverage with two distinct colors. Season with sesame seeds and enjoy!

5. This juice is also great accompanied by a pinch of salt and a grinding of pepper.

Difficulty: MEDIUM
Preparation: **10 minutes**
Calories: **113 kcal**

Recipe Properties:
The Spinach Juice with Lemon and Sesame Seeds is a beverage rich in substances that keep the immune system working efficiently and prevent degenerative and vascular diseases. It has a high satiety index, low calorie content and promotes weight loss.

Spinach, *due to its contents of oxalic acid, can favor kidney stones and lower vitamin C concentrations. Hence, it is important always to consume it with a few drops of lemon juice. It contains vitamin A, folic acid (which promotes red blood cell production) and a discreet quantity of minerals. The belief that it is extremely rich in iron does not really reflect reality. It has laxative, cardiotonic and invigorating properties.*
Lemon *neutralizes toxic chemical compounds such as nitrates and facilitates digestion.*
Sesame seeds *can help the immune system during recovery after physical activity and illness.*

2 servings

3 zucchini
1 celery heart

2 organic lemons
6 mint tufts
salt and pepper (optional)

ZUCCHINI, CELERY AND LEMON JUICE WITH MINT

1. Wash the zucchini, trim the ends and cut into pieces small enough for the centrifugal juicer. Clean the mint and set it aside.

2. Clean the celery and remove any damaged parts. Trim the ends then cut into pieces and add to the zucchini. Celery leaves have a strong aroma that tends to overpower other flavors. Therefore, use it in moderation.

3. Wash the lemons, remove most of the rind and cut into pieces small enough for the centrifugal juicer.

4. Extract the juice first from the harder ingredients and then those that are softer. In this case, start with the celery, then the zucchini and finally, the lemon.

5. By extracting the juice from the ingredients separately, you will obtain color and foam effects that are very pleasant to the eye!

6. Before serving, season to taste and decorate with mint tufts.

Difficulty: EASY
Preparation: **7 minutes**
Calories: **44 kcal**
per serving

Recipe Properties:
The Zucchini, Celery and Lemon Juice with Mint is an ideal cocktail for prevention of age-related degenerative diseases, particularly those related to eyesight, and age-related maculopathy. It contains a series of strong antioxidants for defense against free radicals in all body tissues.

Lemon *favors the absorption of iron by the intestine and promotes the healing of wounds.*
Celery *has a good anti-inflammatory action in addition to aiding digestion, and helps combat intestinal gas.*
Zucchini *is an easily digestible vegetable that is low in calories and very rich in water (equal to 94% of its weight), minerals (potassium, iron, calcium and phosphorus), vitamins (A, C, B1 and B2) and bioflavonoids.*
Mint *is a digestive herbaceous plant. Some of the minerals contained in this aromatic herb include calcium, potassium, copper, manganese, sodium and phosphorus. The vitamins include vitamins A, C and D, and B-group vitamins. Amino acids are also abundant in this plant.*

2 servings

1 cucumber
2 small bell peppers (one red and one yellow)

1 fresh red chili pepper
1 tsp. extra virgin olive oil
1 tsp. vinegar
salt

SPICY JUICE WITH BELL PEPPERS, CUCUMBER AND CHILI PEPPER

1. Clean all the vegetables. Trim the ends of the cucumber, and the stems from the bell and chili peppers.

2. Cut the cucumber into pieces and set aside.

3. Chop the bell peppers into pieces, and remove the white parts and the seeds.

4. Cut the chili pepper into rounds.

5. Juice the vegetables separately in a centrifugal juicer to obtain a juice that displays gradations of colors.

6. It is a refreshing and highly thirst-quenching beverage. Perfect during hot days, it can also be used as a sauce for salads and raw vegetables.

Difficulty: EASY
Preparation: **10 minutes**
Calories: **75 kcal**
per serving

Recipe Properties:

The Spicy Juice with Bell Peppers, Cucumber and Chili Pepper promotes weight loss because it is low in calories but filling, and because the spicy flavor of chili pepper speeds up the metabolism and energy expenditure. It is particularly suitable for warm or very humid climates.

Cucumber is rich in water and hence, diuretic and detoxifying. It contains minerals such as calcium, potassium, and phosphorus; and vitamins, particularly vitamins A, C and B-group vitamins. It is very helpful for the kidneys and for combatting constipation. However, not everyone can digest it.
Bell pepper contains a lot of water, abundant fiber and a lot of vitamin C (more than cabbage or spinach). All the pepper varieties are rich in carotenoids and antioxidants.
Chili pepper contains antioxidant bioflavonoids, a lot of vitamin C, and capsaicin, a compound that plays an important role in the prevention of prostate cancer and as an intestinal anti-fermentative.

MIXED FRUIT AND VEGETABLE JUICES, EMULSIONS AND SMOOTHIES

WELL-BALANCED COMBINATIONS

by Cinzia Trenchi

Mixing fruit and vegetables is no longer a taboo. Today, it is not unusual to see combinations that are at times very bold but that in the end reward us with new and interesting flavors. What is important, as always, is to maintain a good balance between the textures, and the sweet, bitter or sour flavors of the various ingredients. In this section, you will find many ideas for delicious snacks with which to calm hunger pangs felt when trying to lose a few extra pounds.

In these pages, there are many suggestions for preparing smoothies and juices that are pleasant, thirst-quenching, interesting for their properties and naturally, easy and quick to make. Bell pepper, lemons and apples; fennel and pears; avocado, celery and lime: do these seem like tasty combinations to you? They are indeed, but they are also refreshing and light blends that can be a healthy snack or transform themselves into an aperitif or an original dish for a summer lunch. The qualities that a juice or a smoothie embodies are many... above all, there are the colors, which in freshly made beverages remain unaltered and appear even to be heightened by the preparation process; if several ingredients are used, by extracting the juice separately, you can experiment creating new color gradations that are different every time. Then, there are the textures: if for a smoothie, the result is a homogeneous mixture, for juices the result is a compact and soft foam that forms over the liquid, onto which spices, seeds or aromatic herbs can be rested with ease. Before drinking, it is sufficient to gently mix the drink to obtain a perfectly blended beverage. Grapes and lettuce, artichokes and dandelion, oranges and celeriac or daikon: these are precisely the kind of ideas that allow to combine a great quantity of vegetables that would be difficult to eat all at once.

A suggestion: for flavors that are farthest from personal preferences, it is best to take a gradual approach and use spices, salt and lemon juice to attenuate them.

DETOXIFYING AND CLEANSING

by Maurizio Cusani

Mixed fruit and vegetable beverages are an elegant and balanced solution for getting a relatively quick energy boost without burdening the digestive system too much. They can be used in different ways to improve our wellbeing. The practice of juice fasting, popular in Anglo-Saxon countries, is considered detoxifying and can successfully be used for short periods to reach specific goals in standardized pro-grams that range from three to nine consecutive days, with the goal, for example, of losing weight or improving the condition of the skin before ceremonies or events of particular personal importance. There are even tailored programs that foresee the preparation of smoothies and juices (blends of cucumbers, pineapples, lemon and chili pepper and so on) for combatting imperfections such as cellulite.

Another possibility is fasting, always under medical observation and with a depurative or esthetic goal, for short periods (for a duration ranging from one to three days) interspersed with consumption of mixed smoothies, in order to quickly lose weight immediately prior to a special occasion. In this case, ingredients such as apples, spinach, pears, cabbage, leaf vegetables and ginger or chili pepper are used. Another interesting choice is to dedicate an entire day to purification, allow-ing the organs of the digestive system to rest by consuming only juices, smoothies and juice concentrates, without mixing them with anything else, and repeating the process a couple of days later.

For a boost of energy in the morning, stimulating beverages such as tea and coffee should be avoided in favor of a simple concentrate of chloroform, the green pigment in vegetables that oxygenates the blood and activates the brain, together with fruit such as grapes and citrus fruit. To aid in weight-loss diets and placate the appetite during the day, mixed smoothies or juices with ingredients such as apples, pears, celery, fennel and spices are ideal. Finally, to recharge or relax after a day of work, spinach, broccoli, celery, carrots, citrus fruit and wild berries are perfect.

2 servings

1 celery heart
1 avocado
1 lime

salt
1 tsp. celery seeds
pepper (optional)

AVOCADO DIP
WITH CELERY SEEDS AND LIME

1. Wash and dry the celery.

2. Peel the avocado, remove the pit, cut the pulp into pieces and place into the blender jar.

3. Cut the lime into halves, set a slice aside to use for decoration and juice the rest. Pour the juice over the avocado.

4. Add a pinch of salt and pepper if desired, and blend.

5. Pour the resulting cream into a bowl. Decorate with a slice of lime and the celery seeds. Serve it with celery sticks and enjoy.

6. This blend is perfect as a light and tasty appetizer.

Difficulty: EASY
Preparation: **7 minutes**
Calories: **160 kcal**
per serving

Recipe Properties:
The Avocado Dip with Celery Seeds and Lime is low in calories and high in antioxidants. Suitable for all ages, it has a very pleasant taste. In addition, it is particularly useful to people suffering from cardiovascular disease. It also has a high satiety index.

Avocado, *contains many unsaturated fats and Omega 3, which act as antioxidants, and helps prevent tumors (particularly in the mouth) and vascular disease. Compounds contained in this fruit increase "good" cholesterol (HDL) and lower "bad" cholesterol (LDL).*
Lime *effectively lowers cholesterol levels in the blood. In fact, it has been found that the levels of ApoB, secreted by liver cells and typically high in subjects with high cholesterol, fall dramatically if lime is consumed with meals.*
Celery *is diuretic, slimming, combats water retention and is a valid ally in the fight against cellulite.*

1 serving 1/2 grapefruit 3 1/2 oz. (100 g) avocado
3 1/2 oz. (100 g) papaya

PAPAYA AND AVOCADO SMOOTHIE WITH GRAPEFRUIT JUICE

1. Remove the seeds and the skin from the papaya and the avocado, and cut them into pieces.

2. Juice the grapefruit. Catch the juice and pour it into the blender jar. Add the papaya and avocado, and blend as long as necessary to obtain a smooth and homogeneous mixture.

3. Pour into a glass and drink immediately.

4. This nutritious and energetic beverage is perfect before physical activity or as breakfast on a busy morning.

Difficulty: EASY
Preparation: **5 minutes**
Calories: **243 kcal**

Recipe Properties:
The Papaya and Avocado Smoothie with Grapefruit Juice is rich in antioxidants, compounds useful for preserving blood vessel elasticity, particularly of the capillaries, and slowing the ageing of arteries and senses (eyesight, hearing, etc.).

Papaya *contains important antioxidants such as vitamin E and essential minerals such as iron, phosphorus and calcium. It is rich in papain, a digestive enzyme of fundamental importance to the digestive system, and in flavonoids, which regularize blood vessel permeability, a vital aspect of microcirculation.*
Grapefruit *is a natural antibiotic and thirst-quencher recommended when suffering from ear infections or sore throats caused by frequent passage between the hot outdoor and air-conditioned indoor environments.*
Avocado *contains large amounts of vitamins A and E, lutein and glutathione, which are antioxidants excellent for preventing the aging of body tissues.*

2 servings   10 1/2 oz. (300 g) grapes   1 fennel
                        1 orange

GRAPE SMOOTHIE WITH FENNEL AND ORANGE JUICE

1. Wash the grapes. Detach the berries from the stalk and if you prefer a smoother beverage, cut them into halves and remove the seeds.

2. Peel the orange, remove the white portions and separate the wedges.

3. Wash the fennel and cut into pieces small enough for a masticating or centrifugal juicer. Juice it together with the orange.

4. Transfer the juice into the blender jar together with the grapes. Blend as long as necessary to obtain a smooth and foamy mixture.

5. Divide among glasses and drink immediately.

Difficulty: EASY
Preparation: **10-15 minutes**
Calories: **115 kcal**
per serving

Recipe Properties:

The Grape Smoothie with Fennel and Orange Juice is a summer and fall beverage that is very rich in antioxidants and energizing substances. Recommended for speeding up recovery even after intense physical activity, it is thirst-quenching, promotes weight loss and has a pleasant aroma.

Orange is famous for keeping away colds and the flu. However, it is also recommended to individuals with heart problems and high blood pressure; above all, because of its hesperidin content, a compound contained in all citrus fruit, which greatly helps maintain the elasticity of capillaries.
Fennel is an herbaceous plant that is very rich in vitamins (above all, vitamin A) and minerals (potassium, calcium and phosphorus), compounds that are fundamental for athletes and the digestive system.
Grapes contain large amounts of B-group vitamins, particularly B1, B2 and PP, and vitamins A and C. They have regenerative powers, help maintain a sense of well-being and keep the digestive system working properly.

2 servings

2 organic oranges
1 lemon

10 1/2 oz. (300 g) celeriac
1 tsp. cardamom pods

CITRUS FRUIT JUICE WITH CELERIAC AND CARDAMOM

1. Wash the oranges, peel them and remove the white membranes coating the wedges. Set aside a piece of the peel to centrifuge with the other ingredients.

2. Peel the celeriac. Wash, dry and cut it into pieces small enough for the centrifugal juicer.

3. Peel the lemon, remove the white portions and separate the wedges.

4. Extract the juice from the ingredients in a centrifugal juicer and divide among glasses. Place the piece of orange peel into the centrifugal juicer and run it. Add it to every glass so that its aroma infuses the surface of the juice.

5. Crush the cardamom pods, add 2 or 3 to each glass and serve immediately.

Difficulty: EASY
Preparation: **10 minutes**
Calories: **80 kcal**
per serving

Recipe Properties:
The Citrus Fruit Juice with Celeriac and Cardamom is low in calories and thirst-quenching. It rapidly replenishes minerals after intense physical activity and greatly helps prevent cold season illnesses.

Citrus fruit are rich in vitamins C and E, minerals and anti-ageing antioxidants. They are all low in calories, depurative and serve to cleanse and protect our bodies from cold season illnesses.
Cardamom is a spice widely used in traditional Chinese medicine for treating oral cavity, dental or gum conditions. It improves bad breath and helps regularize the working of the gastro-intestinal tract.
Celeriac has depurative and diuretic properties. It is rich in fiber, low in calories and has significant amounts of vitamins and antioxidants.

2 servings

7 oz. (200 g) baked beets
2 organic apples
1 tsp. sunflower seeds

1 tsp. vinegar
salt and pepper

BEET AND APPLE JUICE WITH SUNFLOWER SEEDS

1. Toast the seeds in a non-stick frying pan for a few minutes to render them easier to digest.

2. Peel the beet, cut it into pieces and place into the juicer. Extract the juice and season immediately with vinegar, salt and pepper.

3. Wash the apples. Cut them into pieces small enough for the juicer. You can leave the pectin-rich skin on.

4. Catch the juice and pour it on top of the beet juice. Stir, add the seeds, decorate as desired with beet or apple pieces and serve immediately.

5. This juice is a perfect aperitif or a filling, extremely satisfying beverage that is nutritious and low in calories.

Difficulty: EASY
Preparation: **5 minutes**
Calories: **160 kcal**
per serving

Recipe Properties:
The Beet and Apple Juice with Sunflower Seeds is thirst-quenching, energizing and low in calories. Excellent for getting your strength back after physical or mental activity, it is also very useful for the prevention of age-related diseases.

Beet has a well-balanced content of proteins, fiber and sugars. It is rich in potassium and vitamins A and C. Its extracts can improve stamina.
Sunflower seeds contain many antioxidant fatty acids, linoleic acid, vitamins A and B, and minerals such as iron, zinc and phosphorus. Excellent for maintaining intestinal health and as protection against vascular disease, they also have a calming effect on the nervous system.
An apple, in addition to its many great properties, can help regularize blood sugar levels.

2 servings

6 carrots
1 green apple
2 lemons

1 Delicious apple for the skewers
edible flowers and aromatic herbs
    for decoration
2 wood skewers

CARROT JUICE
WITH APPLE AND LEMON

1. Wash the herbs and flowers for decoration and place them to dry on paper towels. Clean and peel or grate the carrots. Cut into pieces small enough for the centrifugal juicer and place into the appliance.

2. Wash and peel the green apples, cut into pieces small enough for the centrifugal juicer and add to the carrots.

3. Juice the lemon in a lemon juicer and filter the juice in a strainer to eliminate any seeds.

4. Wash the Delicious apple. Cut it into slices, dip in the lemon juice (in this way, the slices will not turn brown because lemon juice stops oxidation) and string them onto the skewers.

5. Juice the carrots and the apple in the centrifugal juicer, catch the juice and mix with the lemon juice. Divide among glasses, decorate with the skewers and serve immediately.

Difficulty: EASY
Preparation: **5 minutes**
Calories: **160 kcal**
per serving

Recipe Properties:
The Carrot Juice with Apple and Lemon is a helpful aid in strengthening the body's defenses and combatting age-related illnesses due to its antioxidant content. Because it is filling but low in calories, it is a perfect addition to weight-loss diets.

__Carrot__ has digestion-aiding properties and promote intestinal transit. It has significant antioxidant properties and provides a good supply of vitamins, which help keep the eyes and skin healthy. It plays an important role in stimulating the immune system and seems to have an anti-tumor effect as well.
__Apple__ is rich in polyphenols and flavonoids, which have anti-aging and rejuvenating properties. It is very helpful to constipation sufferers and in weight-loss diets.
__Lemon__ stimulates the appetite, strengthens the immune system and supports the body's self-regenerating ability.

2 servings

4 carrots
1 mango
4 fresh oregano sprigs

2 small lime branches for
  decoration
2 tbsp. lemon juice (optional)

CARROT AND MANGO JUICE

1. Clean the carrots. Trim the ends and cut into pieces small enough for the centrifugal juicer.

2. Peel the mango and cut it into pieces.

3. Place the ingredients into a centrifugal juicer. Catch the juice, stir it and if you prefer your juice less sweet, add the lemon juice.

4. Divide the beverage among glasses and decorate with aromatic herbs, which will render the juice more pleasant to the eye and tastier to the palate.

Difficulty: EASY
Preparation: **10 minutes**
Calories: **135 kcal**
per serving

Recipe Properties:
The Carrot and Mango Juice is a detoxifying and refreshing beverage. It is rich in antioxidants and acts as a depurative. However, it is also energizing, diuretic and mildly laxative. It is useful in weight-loss diets due to its high satiety index.

Carrot tones and detoxifies the liver, and is a good diuretic and depurative. **Mango** is a tropical fruit of Asian origin that can weigh as much as two pounds (one kilogram). There are numerous mango varieties on the market. However, all have high sugar contents. For this reason, it is not recommended for individuals suffering from kidney disease or diabetes. It also has anti-inflammatory and soothing properties, and is a valid sleeping aid. Because it is composed of over 80% water, it is refreshing, mildly laxative and diuretic.

1 serving   3 black carrots   1/3 cup (50 g) blueberries
1 plum

BLACK CARROT JUICE WITH BLUEBERRIES AND PLUM

1. Wash the carrots, grate them or remove the outer layer with a vegetable peeler.

2. Trim the ends of the carrots and cut into pieces small enough for the masticating juicer.

3. Wash the blueberries and the plum. Cut the plum into pieces eliminating the pit.

4. Extract the juice from the blueberries first, then the carrots and finally, the plum.

5. Pour into a glass and drink immediately because the beverage will oxidize rapidly.

6. This marvelously colored juice is topped by an irresistible foam, which concentrates the lighter hues of the blueberries and the plum.

Difficulty: EASY
Preparation: **10 minutes**
Calories: **102 kcal**

Recipe Properties:
The Black Carrot Juice with Blueberries and Plum is an antioxidant-rich beverage that helps keep the eyesight, heart and circulation working properly. It is a healthy boost of energy for overcoming periods of depression and bouts of constipation.

Black carrot *(or purple carrot) is rich in vitamin A and fiber. It has antioxidant properties very similar to those of blueberries because of its contents of anthocianosides, which help prevent microcirculatory disorders. It is a good anti-inflammatory and helps protect the eyesight. In fact, the typical orange color of this root was only developed in the 1600s, by the Dutch, in honor of William of Orange, who lead the struggle for Dutch independence. Currently, carrots are cultivated in a variety of colors.*
Blueberry *(as well as lingonberry and bilberry) is rich in anthocianosides, which have antioxidant properties and help keep circulation healthy.*
Plum *is an important fruit for dulling the sense of hunger and eliminating slag from the intestine.*

1 organic green apple
6 cabbage leaves
3 1/2 oz. (100 g) cauliflower

salt, chili pepper, lemon juice
(optional)

CABBAGE, CAULIFLOWER AND APPLE JUICE

1. Wash the apple. Remove the core and the seeds, and cut into pieces. Keep the skin on.

2. Soak the cabbage leaves and cauliflower in cold water for a few minutes. Cut the leaves into pieces small enough for the juicer. Do not remove the harder fluid-rich sections.

3. Cut the inflorescences into pieces and juice the ingredients separately.

4. The apple juice will tend to sink to the bottom, the cabbage juice will remain in the middle, and the cauliflower juice will rest on top covered by a delicate foam.

5. This juice makes it possible to use raw Brassicaceae vegetables and improves their flavor through the addition of apple juice.

6. If desired, you can season the juice with salt, chili pepper and lemon.

Difficulty: EASY
Preparation: **5 minutes**
Calories: **108 kcal**

Recipe Properties:
The Cabbage, Cauliflower and Apple Juice is a healthy beverage that is an excellent aid in the battle against age-related degenerative diseases. In addition to its beneficial effects on intestinal transit, some consider it an excellent food for the prevention of digestive tract tumors.

***Cauliflower** is recommended for diabetics because its properties help regularize blood sugar levels. It also helps prevent colon cancer and ulcers. It is very helpful in the treatment of anemia due to its contents of antioxidants (flavones) and indole, substances capable of defending against the ageing actions of free radicals. Its juice can help prevent colds and the flu.*
***Cabbage** is a typical winter vegetable. The parts of the vegetable used for consumption include the green leaves and inflorescences (broccoli). Its protein and low calorie contents make it a recommended ingredient in diets.*
***Apple** improves memory and has beneficial effects on the skin. It is low in calories and conducive to weight loss.*

2 servings

1 red or Tropea onion
1 cucumber
2 cups (300 g) small ripe
  tomatoes (cherry or similar)
1 tsp. extra virgin olive oil

1 tsp. apple vinegar
salt
1/2 tsp. chili powder
2 tufts or sprigs lemon beebrush
  for aroma and decoration

CUCUMBER AND ONION JUICE, AND TOMATO SMOOTHIE

1. Peel the onion. Cut it into pieces small enough for the centrifugal juicer. Wash the cucumber and set aside 2 slices to use for decoration.

2. Peel the rest of the cucumber, add it to the onion and extract the juice. Catch it in a glass and pour it into the blender jar.

3. Wash the tomatoes. Cut into pieces allowing them to fall directly into the blender. Add the oil, vinegar, salt and chili pepper.

4. Blend the ingredients until a homogeneous emulsion is obtained (normally, a few tens of seconds are sufficient!). Pour into glasses and decorate with the lemon beebrush.

5. It is a magnificent blend for satisfying hunger or quenching thirst with a decidedly appetizing emulsion.

Difficulty: EASY
Preparation: **10 minutes**
Calories: **90 kcal**
per serving

Recipe Properties:
The Cucumber and Onion Juice, and Tomato Smoothie is an excellent aid to weight loss because it is low in calories and very filling. It has many antioxidants useful for combatting degenerative diseases of all tissue types.

__Tomato__ can greatly help loose weight. However, it should not be consumed by individuals who are allergic to plants of the nightshade family (potatoes, eggplants and peppers).
__Cucumber__, with its high water content, is an excellent diuretic and detoxifyer. It contains essential minerals such as calcium, potassium and phosphorus; as well as vitamins A and C, and B-group vitamins. This vegetable is very useful to the kidneys and helps with constipation. However, not everyone can digest it. Due to its sulfur content, it was also used to treat intestinal worms in ancient times.
__Onion__ is low in calories, and ideal for individuals suffering from high blood pressure or circulatory diseases.

1 serving

1/2 cup (100 g) baby
  spinach
1 lemon
7 oz. (200 g) daikon
salt and pepper (optional)

Difficulty: MEDIUM
Preparation: **10-15 minutes**
Calories: **78 kcal**

DAIKON, SPINACH AND LEMON JUICE

1. Soak the spinach in cold water. Rinse several times to eliminate any residual dirt. Drain and remove the roots and damaged leaves. Set a few leaves aside to use for decoration.

2. Peel the lemon. Remove the white portions as well. Cut into pieces small enough for the centrifugal blender.

3. Wash the daikon, cut it into pieces and set a few aside for juice presentation.

4. In a centrifugal juicer, extract the juice first from the lemon, then the daikon and finally, from the spinach.

5. Decorate the beverage with the spinach leaves and the pieces of daikon.

6. If desired, you can season the juice with salt and pepper.

Recipe Properties:
The Daikon, Spinach and Lemon Juice is an excellent aid to digestion. It is low on calories, thirst-quenching, slimming and filling. It has a positive effect on liver function and is very useful to individuals with intestinal problems or stomach gas.

*Daikon or **Oriental radish** or **white radish** is a root of Japanese origin that looks like a large carrot and has a sharp, spicy flavor. It promotes the digestion of fats and difficult to digest foods, has significant diuretic and hepatoprotective properties, and is a fair mucolytic. It is low in calories but stimulates the appetite and is recommended in the first trimester of pregnancy, the period during which nausea is very frequent. **Spinach** has laxative, cardiotonic and invigorating properties.*

1 serving

1 fennel
1 pear
1 lemon
fennel leaves
 for decoration

Difficulty: EASY
Preparation: **10 minutes**
Calories: **60 kcal**

FENNEL, PEAR AND LEMON JUICE

1. Soak the fennel in cold water for a few minutes. Strip the leaves and remove any ruined external layers. Cut into pieces small enough for a centrifugal juicer.

2. Peel the pear and cut into pieces.

3. Juice the lemon in a lemon juicer or, if you prefer, peel it, remove the white portions and separate into wedges.

4. Place all of the ingredients into a centrifugal juicer. Catch the juice, stir and drink immediately.

5. Refreshing, light and delicious! This is a fantastic beverage with very few calories!

Fennel combats stomach gas and is very useful during menopause because it helps regularize female hormones. Fennel juice facilitates the onset of lactation.
Pear is rich in potassium, has a high satiety index and is perfect for individuals with high blood pressure. It contains a lot of water, fiber and a large dose of antioxidant vitamins.
Lemon is a natural disinfectant: a few drops of lemon juice quickly eliminate 92% of microbes and bacteria on the surface of oysters. The addition of lemon juice can disinfect and render potable a quart (1 liter) of water.

Recipe Properties:
The Fennel, Pear and Lemon Juice is a healthy beverage, particularly beneficial to individuals with circulatory disorders or high blood pressure. Low in calories and prone to weight loss, it is also useful for facilitating intestinal transit and combatting degenerative diseases.

2 servings   2 cups (300 g) grapes   1 head of lettuce

LETTUCE AND GRAPE JUICE

1. Wash the grapes and detach the berries from the stalk.

2. Soak the lettuce in water. Remove any ruined leaves then gently drain. Detach the leaves from the core but do not throw it away.

3. In a centrifugal juicer or a juicing press, extract the juice first from the grapes and then the lettuce (leaves and core cut into pieces).

4. A soft suspension will form over the heavier liquid. It will blend with the juice once delicately stirred.

Difficulty: EASY
Preparation: **15 minutes**
Calories: **110 kcal**
per serving

Recipe Properties:
The Lettuce and Grape Juice is very refreshing and suitable for weight-loss diets. Useful for healthy digestion, it is mildly laxative, hydrating, thirst-quenching and rich in minerals. It helps control moodiness in children.

Grapes contain vitamins, essential minerals such as potassium, magnesium, phosphorus and calcium, fiber, organic acids and very important antioxidants. Lettuce is low in calories and consists mostly of water (90-95% of the total weight) and fiber; it is refreshing, diuretic and mildly laxative. Extremely rich in minerals (such as potassium, calcium, phosphorus, iron), vitamins C, E and K, B-group vitamins and carotenoids. It is highly recommended for intestinal health and weight-loss diets. It aids sleep in children but can also cause air swallowing.

1 serving

1 red onion
1 fresh chili pepper

4 mandarin oranges

MANDARIN ORANGE, ONION AND CHILI PEPPER JUICE

1. Peel the onion then cut it into pieces small enough for a juicing press or a centrifugal juicer.

2. Wash the chili pepper. Eliminate the stem, the seeds and the white portions. (The seeds and white portions are often very spicy. Removing them reduces the spiciness!)

3. Peel the mandarin oranges and divide them into wedges.

4. In a centrifugal juicer, first juice the onion, then the chili pepper and finally, the mandarin oranges.

5. The juice will separate forming a deposit on the bottom and a light, aromatic foam on the surface. Stir the mixture before drinking to enjoy a truly pleasant mix of flavors in which the sweet, the spicy and the aromatic blends to create an original, highly thirst-quenching beverage.

Difficulty: EASY
Preparation: **8 minutes**
Calories: **121 kcal**

Recipe Properties:
The Mandarin Orange, Onion and Chili Pepper Juice promotes weight loss, stimulates the metabolism by consuming fats and is depurative. Rich in vitamins and antioxidants, it is also useful for combatting winter illnesses and is an antiseptic.

Mandarin orange *is a fruit that originates in Asia. It is rich in vitamins C and A, and fiber.*
Onion *has significant concentrations of minerals (zinc, potassium, magnesium, phosphorus, etc.) and vitamins (A, C and B-group). It is low in calories, rich in folic acid and considered an excellent detoxicant and depurative, in addition to adequately regularizing gastrointestinal function and facilitating the digestion of simple sugars.*
Chili pepper *protects against infections and improves digestion and circulation.*

1 serving

1 pomegranate
1 piece of ginger root

4 fennel leaves

POMEGRANATE, FENNEL AND GINGER JUICE

1. During preparation of this juice, particular attention must be paid to the amount of ginger used, because the intense flavor of this root can overwhelm those of other ingredients.

2. Open the pomegranate and deseed it. Remove the internal membranes and tease out the seeds.

3. Peel the piece of ginger root (the size of an olive) and add to the pomegranate.

4. Wash the fennel leaves and cut into small pieces.

5. Place the ingredients into the juicer a little at a time and catch the juice. Stir and drink immediately.

6. If you are not used to the flavor of ginger, instead of juicing it with the other ingredients, you can use it to add aroma to the juice by threading it onto a skewer and allowing it to soak in the juice for a few minutes before drinking.

Difficulty: MEDIUM
Preparation: **10 minutes**
Calories: **130 kcal**

Recipe Properties:
The Pomegranate, Fennel and Ginger Juice is highly stimulating, low in calories and diuretic. It helps flush the body and acts as a mild laxative. Rich in antioxidants, it helps fight age-related diseases, quickly restores energy and improves the mood.

Pomegranate is the fruit of the Punica granatum shrub. Its seeds, composed of about 80% water, are diuritic, beneficial to digestion and astringent.
Ginger is a very versatile spice with tonic, anti-inflammatory, fever reducing and mildly antioxidant properties. It is also known as a low-calorie aid to weight-loss diets. It contains B-group vitamins, vitamins C and E, and various minerals such as calcium, magnesium, iron, manganese, zinc, copper and selenium.
Fennel is diuretic, depurative, reduces bloating and satisfies the appetite.

2 servings

2 apples
1 red bell pepper
1 lemon
salt and pepper (optional)

Difficulty: EASY
Preparation: **10 minutes**
Calories: **95 kcal**
per serving

BELL PEPPER, APPLE AND LEMON JUICE

1. Wash the apples, the bell pepper and the lemon.

2. Peel the apples, eliminate the core and cut into pieces.

3. Peel the lemon and separate the wedges. Break the bell pepper into pieces and remove the white portions, the stem and the seeds.

4. Place the ingredients into a juicer. Catch the juice and season with salt and pepper to taste. Divide between two glasses, stir and serve.

5. Refreshing and thirst-quenching, it is a good aperitif in the summer months.

Recipe Properties:
The Bell Pepper, Apple and Lemon Juice is detoxifying, and rich in vitamins and fiber. Above all, it is low in calories, suitable to all weight-loss diets and can help regularize intestinal transit.

Bell pepper contains more vitamin C than citrus fruit (if eaten raw). It also has notable amounts of beta-carotene (mostly in red bell peppers) and various B-group vitamins. These are accompanied by many minerals, such as iron, magnesium, calcium and above all, potassium. Large quantities of water and fiber present produce a mild diuretic and laxative effect making it a very useful ingredient in any weight-loss diet.
Apple contains large quantities of fiber, which is very important to the healthy functioning of the digestive tract.

2 servings

1 yellow grapefruit
1 pomegranate
1 piece of ginger
2 cinnamon sticks
1 pizzico di cannella in
  polvere

Difficulty: MEDIUM
Preparation: **10 minutes**
Calories: **90 kcal**
per serving

GRAPEFRUIT, POMEGRANATE CINNAMON AND GINGER JUICE

1. Peel the grapefruit, remove the white membrane coating the slices and divide into wedges.

2. Open the pomegranate and tease out the seeds. Remove any remnant membranes and gather the seeds into a bowl.

3. Peel a piece of ginger the size of a hazelnut. If you like its aroma, you can use a bigger piece of the root.

4. Juice the pomegranate seeds, ginger and finally, the grapefruit in a centrifugal juicer.

5. Aromatize with a pinch of cinnamon, stir, pour into glasses and decorate with pieces of ginger and cinnamon sticks.

Pomegranate is diuretic, detoxifying and composed of 80% water.
Cinnamon is a spice with antioxidant properties. It has antiseptic, antibacterial and antispasmodic properties. Due to its trypsin contents, it is an important aid in the elimination of fats from the bloodstream and control of blood sugar levels. It also combats intestinal fermentation and reduces the sense of hunger. Recent studies have also hypothesized its role in combatting neurologic deceases and dementia.
Grapefruit is considered an excellent low-calorie fruit. Thanks to its capacity to stimulate lymphatic vessels, it helps flush excess liquids and fats out of the body.

Recipe Properties:
The Grapefruit, Pomegranate, Cinnamon and Ginger Juice is a low-calorie, slimming beverage that lowers the appetite, interacts directly with the nervous system and speeds up the metabolism. It also has excellent health benefits due to its high contents of vitamins and antioxidants.

1 serving

1 small organic green apple
5 radishes
1 cucumber
salt and apple vinegar
    (optional)

Difficulty: EASY
Preparation: **5 minutes**
Calories: **95 kcal**

RADISH, CUCUMBER AND APPLE JUICE

1. Wash the apple and cut into pieces, with the skin on.

2. Clean the radishes, remove the leaves and the roots, and cut into 2 or 4 pieces depending on the size needed.

3. Wash the cucumber, peel two thirds of its surface (the green skin is a natural colorant and will give the beverage a color of varying intensity depending on the amount used) and cut into pieces.

4. Juice the ingredients separately in a centrifugal juicer. When poured into a glass, they will tend to remain separated.

5. Pour into a glass and drink immediately. If you like, you can season the mixture with salt and apple vinegar.

Recipe Properties:
The Radish, Cucumber and Apple Juice is low in calories, slimming and very filling. It is of great help in the prevention of intestinal and respiratory diseases and promotes the production of red blood cells.

__Apple__ is composed of about 85% water and is low in calories. It is rich in vitamins (C, PP, B1, B2, A) and contains malic acid (about 0.2-0.5 ounces, 0.6-1.3 grams).
__Cucumber__ is composed mostly of water and is therefore an excellent diuretic and detoxifier. It contains minerals such as calcium, potassium and phosphorus; and vitamins A, C and B-group vitamins. It is a great aid to proper kidney function and against constipation.
__Radish__ is an excellent bronchodilator, expectorant, antibacterial and antianemic. It has a good quantity of vitamins C and K, B-group vitamins, and iron.

1 serving

1 tomato
4 radishes
1 lemon
salt and pepper
spices, pods of cardamom
  (optional)

Difficulty: EASY
Preparation: **8 minutes**
Calories: **56 kcal**

RADISH, LEMON AND TOMATO JUICE

1. Wash the tomato. Remove the stem and any hard portions. Cut it into small pieces.

2. Clean the radishes, remove the leaves and the roots. Cut into 2 or 4 pieces.

3. Extract the juice from a lemon and catch it into a glass.

4. Juice the tomato and the radishes in a centrifugal juicer. Removing the skin and seeds from the tomato will result in a particularly smooth juice, which is recommended for those who find small bits in their beverages unpleasant.

5. Season with salt, pepper and, if desired, with spices or cardamom pods.

Radish contains a lot of vitamins, minerals and antioxidants, which produce its typical red color. Its leaves are also rich in minerals and can be used together with other vegetables to prepare excellent salads.
Lemon, a citrus fruit of Asian origin that has integrated perfectly into the Mediterranean, continues to ripen when removed from the tree prematurely.
Tomato is of fundamental importance to individuals with high blood pressure or gouty arthritis. It also has acne-fighting properties and improves skin elasticity.

Recipe Properties:
The Radish, Lemon and Tomato Juice is low in calories and slimming. It effectively contributes to the reintroduction of minerals and water after intense physical activity. Its substantial antioxidant content greatly contributes to staying healthy.

2 servings

1 white celery
1 apple
2 carrots
4 thyme sprigs

4 sage leaves
4 chive stalks
edible flowers for decorating

CELERY AND APPLE JUICE WITH AROMATIC HERBS AND CHIVES

1. Clean the aromatic herbs and the celery.

2. Remove the leaves and the dark or ruined sections from the celery. Cut into pieces and transfer to a centrifugal juicer.

3. Wash the carrots. Peel or grate them, as you prefer, then cut and add to the celery.

4. Wash the apple and cut it into halves. Set aside 2 slices to use for decoration, peel the rest of the apple and cut into small pieces.

5. Add the apple to the celery and carrots, and extract the juice.

6. Pour the juice into glasses, add aroma with chopped chives and finish with the herbs, apple slices and edible flowers.

7. Serve immediately to fully enjoy the health benefits of the fresh fruit and vegetables.

Difficulty: EASY
Preparation: **10 minutes**
Calories: **120 kcal**
per serving

Recipe Properties:
The Celery and Apple Juice with Aromatic Herbs and Chives, in addition to being low in calories and conducive to weight loss, is depurative, antiseptic and contains numerous antioxidants that prevent age-related degenerative diseases, particularly cardiovascular diseases.

Celery contains potassium, calcium, phosphorus, magnesium, selenium and good quantities of vitamins A, C and K.
Carrot protects the arteries and fortifies the immune system.
Chive is a hardy perennial plant with edible leaves that are harvested throughout the year. It has excellent depurative and antiseptic properties, stimulates the appetite and the production of gastric acids, and is mildly laxative. Because it has a tonic effect on the heart, it has been considered aphrodisiac by some. In addition, it contains vitamin C, phosphorus and potassium.
Aromatic herbs are excellent sources of vitamins, minerals and fiber.

1 serving

1 cup (200 g) spinach
5 radishes
5 walnuts
1 organic lemon

Difficulty: EASY
Preparation: **10 minutes**
Calories: **123 kcal**

RADISH, SPINACH, WALNUT AND LEMON JUICE

1. Clean the spinach, let it soak in cold water then gently dry the leaves and set a few aside.

2. Wash the radishes, remove the leaves and cut into halves or quarters.

3. Wash the lemon, remove some of the rind (leave about 1/4 on) and cut the citrus fruit into small pieces.

4. Shell the walnuts (set 2 kernels aside to use for decoration) and crush them in a mortar obtaining a homogeneous flour.

5. Transfer the vegetables and the lemon into a centrifugal juicer. Divide the resulting juice among glasses, season with the walnut flour and stir. Decorate with spinach leaves and walnut kernels, and drink immediately in order to enjoy the refreshing flavor of the ingredients at its best.

Lemon is a valid ally in the fight against cellulite.
Walnut is rich in Omega 3 fatty acids. It protects the heart and helps prevent eye disease. It contains vitamin B and the minerals calcium and potassium. Walnut has anti-aging, anti-degenerating properties and helps regulate cholesterol levels.
Radish contains many vitamins, minerals and antioxidants.
Spinach has vitamin A, folic acid and a discrete amount of minerals..

Recipe Properties:
The Radish, Spinach, Walnut and Lemon Juice, in addition to being useful in weight-loss diets, is rich in antioxidants such as Omega 3 and 6, vitamin C and flavonoids, which protect against cancer and degenerative diseases.

1 serving

1/2 cup (100 g) common
   dandelion
1 lemon
1 artichoke
salt and pepper

Difficulty: MEDIUM
Preparation: **10-15 minutes**
Calories: **69 kcal**

COMMON DANDELION, ARTICHOKE AND LEMON JUICE

1. Soak the dandelion in cold water to remove any residual dirt then drain.

2. Extract the juice from the lemon and set aside.

3. Clean the artichoke, remove any damaged leaves and peel the stem. Place into a juicer together with the dandelion and extract the juice. Add the lemon juice, season with salt and pepper, and serve.

4. The predominant taste is bitter, which is attenuated by the lemon juice. Because of its unusual flavor, it is best to start with small amounts!

The **common dandelion** or **blow ball** or **lion's tooth** is a very common herbaceous perennial plant that can be found at elevations as high as 5,900 feet (1800 meters). It is best if harvested before it flowers, in February or September, when the plant is most tender and retains all of its properties. Specifically, it is rich in polyphenols and is a diuretic.
Lemon is an excellent nasal decongestant. It protects against infection and keeps the oral cavity healthy. It also has many other properties: it prevents arteriosclerosis and has a benefic effect on the liver and the pancreas.
Artichoke is of great help in reducing fat and cholesterol levels in the blood and in keeping the blood vessel walls elastic.

Recipe Properties:
The Common Dandelion, Artichoke and Lemon Juice is a healthy beverage with diuretic properties that is ideal for individuals with elevated levels of fats and cholesterol in the blood. Low in calories and slimming, it is also an excellent aid to the proper functioning of the liver.

129

1 serving

1 zucchini
1 lemon
1/2 tsp. spice mix: pepper,
   cardamom, cinnamon, coriander

1 tsp. extra virgin olive oil
salt

ZUCCHINI AND LEMON JUICE WITH SPICES

1. Wash the zucchini, trim the ends and cut into pieces small enough for the masticating juicer.

2. Cut the lemon into halves and set aside a slice to use for decoration.

3. Peel the citrus fruit, cut it into pieces and juice it together with the zucchini.

4. Pour the juice into a glass, season with salt and spices, stir and drink immediately.

Difficulty: EASY
Preparation: **5 minutes**
Calories: **78 kcal**

Recipe Properties:
The Zucchini and Lemon Juice with Spices is extremely low in calories and very filling. It is perfect for keeping the intestine healthy and has many antioxidants such as bioflavonoids and anti-aging compounds.

Zucchini is an easily digestible vegetable that is extremely rich in water (94% of its weight). It is low in calories and contains minerals (potassium, iron, calcium and phosphorus), vitamins (A, C, B1 and B2) and bioflavonoids, which are very useful antioxidants. In addition, it contains lutein and zeaxanthin, compounds rarely found in foods that are extremely helpful in the prevention of macular degeneration.
Lemon is used in traditional medicine to keep teeth shiny, white and healthy.
Spices are mineral-rich substances that favor weight loss by accelerating the metabolism.

JUICES, EMULSIONS AND SMOOTHIES WITH VEGETABLE PROTEINS

NATURAL CONSISTENCIES

by Cinzia Trenchi

Smoothies and emulsions with vegetable proteins such as soybeans, rice and oats in the form of milk, cream or yogurt are a valid alternative to animal proteins when following a vegan diet. These ingredients blend perfectly with fruit and vegetables, giving life to extremely tasty preparations. Creaminess and great flavor are the characteristics that become apparent from the very first gulp: whatever the cereal "milk" chosen, the result will be excellent; the only thing that matters when choosing among them is your preference. Cases of sensitivity to different ingredients are growing in frequency, which makes it necessary to diversify one's diet integrating with other elements. Consequently, the possibility to substitute traditional milk, cream and yogurt with other foods while maintaining the consistencies that would be impossible to achieve with other foods is a welcome development. Soy-based beverages, like those based on rice or oats, are a good alternative to an energizing breakfast, can be an excellent extremely low-calorie snack and easily lend themselves to integrating fruit or vegetable-based preparations without covering the original flavor. When choosing what to prepare, in addition to personal preferences, one should keep in mind any intolerances or allergies that can influence the choice between one preparation or another. For years now, it has been possible to find for sale (if it is not possible to prepare them at home) excellent plant-based substitutes even for yogurt and cream. They allow us not to relegate our most loved dishes to the realm of memory, giving us the possibility to continue enjoying them, diet permitting. In addition, a plant-based creams and yogurts are always lighter with respect to their cow milk-based alternatives, without penalizing the flavor. Therefore, clear the way for health, lightness and the possibility to control our calorie intake, particularly since now a diet, in addition to improving our well-being, can satisfy the palate.

ACTIVATING IMMUNE DEFENSES

by Maurizio Cusani

An adult, on average, has a daily protein requirement of one gram per every kilogram of body weight. A balanced diet foresees the consumption of all the different types of proteins. Ideally, one should consume 50% vegetable proteins and 50% animal proteins.

Excessive consumption of animal proteins can lead to the accumulation of nitrogenous compounds in the body, which can slow the metabolism, lead to kidney overexertion and to an overall increase in the level of toxicity. However, these proteins are less "noble" than animal proteins and do not contain a sufficient amount of essential amino acids, i.e. the substances that the human body is not capable of producing on its own and must acquire through the diet. This is why it is important to pair them judiciously with vegetable proteins in order to ensure a complete and balanced diet.

Mixed protein smoothies are very filling and hence very useful in diets, because they can help reduce the overall daily calorie intake without jeopardizing personal health. They also maintain the immune system active on the one hand and boost the tissue self-repair processes on the other. In addition, there is no denying the positive effect on the metabolism given by the use of spices, and the greater richness and nutritional balance given by the mineral and antioxidant contents ensured by the skillful combination of fruit and vegetables, like those in the preparations proposed in this section.

1 serving

2/3 cup (150 g) soy yogurt
1 tsp. powdered spices: cinnamon,
   coriander, clove, fenugreek,
   pepper etc.

1 tsp. (about 5 g) flax oil
1 pinch of salt

SPICED SOY YOGURT EMULSION

1. This recipe can also be prepared using only a small whisk.

2. Place the ingredients into a bowl and blend until a homogeneous mixture is obtained, then pour into a glass and enjoy.

3. This emulsion with spices is extremely rich in aromas and flavors, in addition to being extremely beneficial to our bodies.

4. It can be stored in the refrigerator and is perfect as an tasty appetizer or satisfying snack.

Difficulty: MEDIUM
Preparation: **5 minutes**
Calories: **138 kcal**

Recipe Properties:
The Spiced Soy Yogurt Emulsion is particularly effective in promoting the metabolism. It also acts as an afrodisiac and is rich in compounds that effectively combat free radicals.

Cinnamon is useful in the protection against flu and in stimulating the immune system. It is particularly important for the wellbeing of the intestines and is a good antibacterial agent.
Cloves are antiseptic, antispasmodic, anti-inflamatory and digestion aiding. The flavonoids contained in this spice are powerful antioxidants, help relieve tooth aches due to their painkilling properties and promote oral health by combatting fungal infections.
Soybeans act on aneurological level to reduce the sense of hunger.
Flax oil contains Omega 3 and 6 fatty acids, which help fight constipation and lower cholesterol.

2 servings

1 artichoke
1/3 cup (100 g) soy cream
1 tsp. lemon juice
salt flakes

1 tsp. extra virgin olive oil
2 tufts of parsely

SOY CREAM EMULSION WITH ARTICHOKE AND LEMON JUICE

1. Wash the artichoke. Remove damaged external leaves, the tips of the leaves, and the beard (or choke), if present. Cut into pieces small enough for the juicer. Extract the juice and catch it into a glass.

2. Wash the parsley. In a container, combine the soy cream, oil, and salt flakes. Gradually add the artichoke juice being careful of the amount added: its taste is rather bitter.

3. Mix with a whisk until a homogeneous mixture is obtained. Add the parsley for some aroma and serve with the remaining artichoke juice on the side, which could be added to the mixture if desired.

4. This emulsion is perfect for adding extra flavor to soups, as a special aperitif or an original appetizer.

Difficulty: MEDIUM
Preparation: **5 minutes**
Calories: **145 kcal**
per serving

Recipe Properties:
The Soy Cream Emulsion with Artichoke and Lemon Juice is low in calories, antiseptic, protects organs of detoxification such as the liver, has anti-ageing properties and effectively fights infections.

Lemon has an aroma that improves concentration.
Artichoke is rich in an antioxidant compound (cynarine) that is particularly abundant if the vegetables are consumed raw.
Parsley is an aromatic herb that is very common in southern Europe, where it originates. It contains fiber, minerals (calcium, potassium, sodium, phosphorus, magnesium, iron, zinc, selenium and manganese) and vitamins (A, C, E, K and B-group) in addition to important antioxidants and substantial quantities of bio-flavonoids, antioxidant compounds that can slow down cellular aging.

2 servings

1 tomato
1 celery heart
1/3 cup (100 g) soy cream
1/3 cup (100 g) soy yogurt

2 tufts of parsley
1 tsp. extra virgin olive oil
1 tsp. lemon juice
salt

SOY CREAM AND TOMATO EMULSION WITH CELERY AND PARSLEY

1. Wash the tomato and remove the skin and seeds.

2. Wash the celery (which will serve to add flavor to the cream) and the parsley. Cut the celery into pieces.

3. Finely chop or blend the tomato. Place it into a bowl with oil, lemon juice, salt, cream or yogurt. Emulsify using a whisk until a homogeneous, soft mixture is obtained.

4. Transfer the mixture into glasses or bowls, decorate with parsley and pieces of celery.

5. This magnificent emulsion rich in light and refreshing summer flavors, can be eaten as a snack or a light appetizer.

Difficulty: MEDIUM
Preparation: **10 minutes**
Calories: **110 kcal**
per serving

Recipe Properties:
The Soy Cream and Tomato Emulsion with Celery and Parsley is very filling and a great ally in combatting intestinal transit problems. It is detoxifying, diuretic and rich in numerous antioxidants that act primarily on the nervous system.

Tomato contains compounds that control sebum excretion and prevent oily skin.
Celery is rich in anti-inflammatory, hydrating and flushing substances and vitamin C. It also contains antioxidant flavonoids such as lutein, zeaxanthin and beta-carotene. Its well-known ability to promote weight-loss is due to the presence of the 3-n-butylphthalide molecule and elevated water contents.
Soybeans are beneficial to muscle tone and reduces fat.
Parsley stimulates digestion and combats gas. It is a good tonic and excellent diuretic.

2 servings

3 1/2 oz. (100 g) tofu
1/3 cup (100 g) tofu cream
1 tbsp. extra virgin olive oil
1 tsp. spice mix: turmeric,
   chili pepper, pepper,
   cumin
1 pinch of saffron pistils

Seasonal vegetables, for example:
2 carrot
1 cucumber
4 radishes
2 celery sticks
3 1/2 oz. (100 g) daikon
4 tomatoes
2 wood skewers

TOFU CREAM EMULSION WITH SPICES AND VEGETABLE SKEWERS

1. Wash the vegetables, clean as necessary and place on paper towels to drain.

2. In a small saucepan over very low heat, melt 1 tablespoon of tofu cream with the spices. This ensures a smooth, grain-free mixture.

3. Finely chop the tofu, emulsify with the remaining cream and extra virgin olive oil. Add the cream and spice mixture, and blend until a homogenous consistency is obtained. Embellish with saffron.

4. Cut the vegetables into pieces and prepare some imaginative skewers.

5. Serve the emulsion as an aperitif or an appetizer; it is a flavorful, light cream perfect for a hot day.

Difficulty: MEDIUM
Preparation: **15 minutes**
Calories: **200 kcal**
per serving

Recipe Properties:
The Tofu Cream Emulsion with Spices and Vegetable Skewers is an extremely filling, energy-rich preparation that stimulates the metabolism, promotes the burning of calories and ensures the assumption of a considerable amount of minerals, fiber and vitamins.

Black pepper *is one of the most widely used spices in the world. It is composed of 6% piperine, a compound that gives it its characteristic flavor, promotes digestion and stimulates the production of endorphins in the brain, which have an antidepressant effect.*
Tofu *is a low calorie soy-based cheese that can be used to accompany any vegetable.*
Vegetables *(celery, carrots, radishes, daikon, cucumber) are rich in vitamins A, C and E, contain flavonoids with antioxidant and anti-degenerative properties and essential minerals such as magnesium and iron. They effectively promote weight loss and are very filling.*

SOY YOGURT AND GRAPE SMOOTHIE

1. Remove the grape berries from the stalk, cut them into halves and remove the seeds.

2. Place the grapes and the soy yogurt into the blender jar.

3. Blend until a smooth, soft and homogeneous mixture is obtained. Fill a glass and drink immediately.

4. When blended yogurt is mixed with fruit, it loses its lightness and becomes an extremely thirst-quenching beverage rich in important nutrients. This smoothie is also excellent with ice.

Difficulty: MEDIUM
Preparation: **5 minutes**
Calories: **133 kcal**

Recipe Properties:

The Soy Yogurt and Grape Smoothie is mildly laxative, reinvigorating and hydrating. It is rich in anthocyanin compounds that help protect against cold season and intestinal illnesses.

***Soybeans** contain polyunsaturated fatty acids such as Omega 3, which protect the cardiovascular system. In addition, they are rich in vitamins B9 and E, and essential minerals such as iron and potassium.*
***Grapes** are recommended for sufferers of weakness, anemia, gout, uric acid buildup, arthritis or varicose veins. It is beneficial to digestion, mildly laxative and strengthens the immune system. Carbolic and tannic acids contained in this fruit have an antiviral activity against herpes. The consumption of grapes is at the foundation of ampelotherapy, which has rejuvenating and detoxifying effects.*

2 servings

3/4 cup + 1 1/2 tbsp. (200 g)
rice milk
14 oz. (400 g) pineapple

10 pitted syruped cherries
4 dried apricots
wood skewers

DRIED APRICOT, CHERRIES IN SYRUP AND RICE MILK SMOOTHIE

1. Heat up the rice milk. Take it off the heat, add the apricots and cherries and allow to rest for about 30 minutes. Pour the mixture into the blender jar and blend until foamy.

2. Peel the pineapple, cut it into pieces and thread onto skewers.

3. Divide the smoothie among glasses and serve with the skewers.

4. It is particularly indicated for a nutritious but at the same time light and thirst-quenching breakfast; it is also a magnificent all-healthy dessert!

5. Dried or syruped fruit is an excellent way to enjoy off-season foods.

Difficulty: MEDIUM
Preparation: **10 minutes**
Calories: **180 kcal**
per serving

Recipe Properties:
The Dried Apricot, Cherries in Syrup and Rice Milk Smoothie is extremely energizing, and has an exquisite taste and a pleasant aroma. It has anti-inflammatory properties and plays an active role in the prevention of respiratory and intestinal viral infections.

Cherry *contains substances with anti-inflammatory and painkilling properties.*
Apricot *has a mild laxative effect due to the presence of sorbitol.*
Pineapple *is filling and an excellent diuretic. It helps digestion and relieves pain.*
Rice milk *is suitable for cow milk intolerant individuals because it is lactose-free. It has discreet amounts of calcium and easily digestible simple sugars. It is rich in polyunsaturated fatty acids.*

1 baby banana or "bananito"
1 pear

1/2 cup (100 ml) soy milk

BANANA, PEAR AND SOY MILK SMOOTHIE

1. Peel the banana and cut it into rounds directly into the blender jar.

2. Peel the pear, and remove the stem and the core. Cut it into small pieces and add to the bananas.

3. Add the soy milk to the other ingredients. Blend briefly until a creamy and smooth mixture is obtained.

4. Pour into a glass and enjoy immediately!

5. Satisfying, creamy and charming, this smoothie is also perfect transformed into a tasty ice cream.

Difficulty: EASY
Preparation: **5 minutes**
Calories: **160 kcal**

Recipe Properties:

The Banana, Pear and Soy Milk Smoothie is a rich beverage with high levels of easily digestible sugars, minerals, fiber and proteins. It is a highly energizing and restorative blend that is very filling and perfect for older individuals.

Banana is very filling, rich in potassium, nutritious, energizing and characterized by several properties that help regularize blood pressure and reduce low-density lipoproteins (LDL or "bad" cholesterol), which are detrimental to arterial health.
Pear burns fats, and helps tone the skin and keep it looking young. It is an excellent remedy for high blood pressure and of great help to intestinal health.
Soybeans contain compounds such as genistein and daidzein, which help regularize the levels of estrogen, the hormone responsible for PMS.

2 servings

2 persimmons
3/4 cup + 1 1/2 tbsp. (200 ml)
   rice milk

1 tsp. grated organic lemon and
   orange zest
1 lemon

PERSIMMON AND RICE MILK SMOOTHIE

1. Wash the persimmons. Remove the stems, skin and any seeds, and place the pulp into the blender jar.

2. Juice the lemon.

3. Add grated citrus zest, lemon juice and rice milk. Blend until a smooth and homogeneous mixture is obtained.

4. Divide among glasses and serve immediately.

5. *Rice milk can be easily prepared by boiling 1 part white or brown rice with 10 parts water for about 1 hour over low heat. Once cooled, it should be filtered through a strainer. If desired, it can be flavored with vanilla or honey.*

Difficulty: EASY
Preparation: **5 minutes**
Calories: **136 kcal**
per serving

Recipe Properties:
The Persimmon and Rice Milk Smoothie is a highly energizing beverage, rich in quick and slow-release sugars. It is useful for regularizing gastrointestinal function and for treating constipation or irritable bowel. However, it is not recommended for diabetics.

Persimmon *protects the liver and colon, fights winter fatigue and is ideal for individuals suffering from weakness, convalescents and those exhausted or just very tired. In addition, it helps regularize intestinal function.*
Rice milk *is gluten-free and contains less proteins, cholesterol, saturated fats and vitamin D with respect to cow milk. In addition, it contains unsaturated fats, minerals and abundant simple sugars. It is a good regulator of intestinal functions suitable for colic sufferers.*

2 servings

1/3 cup (50 g) blackberries
1/3 cup (50 g) strawberries
10 1/2 oz. (300 g)
  pineapple
1/3 cup (100 g) soy yogurt

Difficulty: MEDIUM
Preparation: **12 minutes**
Calories: **145 kcal**
per serving

STRAWBERRY SMOOTHIE WITH BLACKBERRIES AND SOY YOGURT

1. Gently wash the blackberries and strawberries under running water. Remove the stem from the strawberries, extract their juice and pour it into the blender jar (this step allows to eliminate the small seeds present in the berries, which not everybody enjoys).

2. Wash the pineapple, peel it, cut it into small pieces and add to the juice.

3. Add the yogurt and blend until a homogeneous mixture is obtained.

4. Pour into glasses and serve immediately so as not to miss out on the magnificent flavor and health benefits of the fresh fruit.

Strawberry *is filling, rich in water, vitamins e antioxidants. Since the only sugar it contains is fructose, it can be eaten by diabetics.*
Blackberry *is diuretic, thirst-quenching, depurative and can effectively combat microcirculatory disorders while lowering low-density cholesterol (LDL), which is damaging to arteries. Mildly laxative, it also has high concentrations of vitamin B9 and folic acid, which is beneficial to women during pregnancy.*
Soybeans *are a legume rich in vitamin A and minerals such as phosphorus and potassium.*

Recipe Properties:

The Strawberry Smoothie with Blackberries and Soy Yogurt is an antioxidant-rich, refreshing and depurative beverage with anti-inflammatory and painkiller properties. Very well balanced and filling, it is recommended for all diets.

2 servings

4 kiwifruit
3/4 cup + 11/2 tbsp.
  (200 ml) oat cream
1 lemon
1 kiwifruit and 1/2 lemon
  for decoration
10 ice cubes

Difficulty: EASY
Preparation: **7 minutes**
Calories: **165 kcal**
per serving

KIWIFRUIT SMOOTHIE WITH LEMON JUICE AND OAT CREAM

1. Wash and peel the kiwifruit. Cut it into pieces letting them fall directly into the blender jar. Add the oat cream.

2. Juice the lemon. Combine with the other ingredients and add the ice.

3. Turn on the blender and blend until a smooth, chunk-free mixture is obtained.

4. Pour the mixture into glasses and decorate with slices of lemon and pieces of kiwifruit.

5. This is a very thirst-quenching, energizing smoothie with a lightly acidic flavor that is also perfect as a hunger-quenching snack.

Lemon promotes the regeneration of skin and scalp.
Oat is rich in avenanthramides, phenolic compounds that appear to have anti-tumor action. This cereal is the richest in protein (almost 15%) and contains unsaturated fatty acids such as linoleic acid, which is beneficial against cardiovascular disease. Oat flour is beneficial for convalescents and children.
Kiwifruit, a native of New Zealand, has easily diffused throughout Europe with Italy currently boasting the highest production numbers in the world. It is very rich in vitamin C.

Recipe Properties:
The Kiwifruit Smoothie with Lemon Juice and Oat Cream is a beverage that helps protect against viral infections and degenerative diseases. It is slimming, hydrating, detoxifying and highly beneficial in early childhood or for quickly regaining strength after an illness.

2 servings 12/3 cups (400 ml) oat milk 1/2 cup (100 ml) sour cherry
1 vanilla pod syrup

VANILLA OAT MILK SMOOTHIE WITH SOUR CHERRY SYRUP

1. Pour the oat milk into a pan. Add 1 vanilla pod broken into pieces and allow to boil for 10 minutes. Allow to cool and filter the milk through a strainer.

2. Once flavored, oat milk can be stored in the refrigerator for some days.

3. Pour the flavored milk into the blender jar, add the sour cherry syrup and blend.

4. This beverage can be stored in the refrigerator for some days without the flavor being affected.

5. This smoothie is very simple to make and can be prepared with any leftover fruit syrup.

Difficulty: MEDIUM
Preparation: **30 minutes**
Calories: **145 kcal**
per serving

Recipe Properties:
The Vanilla Oat Milk Smoothie with Sour Cherry Syrup is a beverage rich in antioxidants (flavonoids and anthocyanids). It is detoxifying and mildly laxative. In addition, it is energizing and reduces psychophysical stress.

Sour cherry *helps regularize cardiovascular activity and has a positive effect on the central nervous system. It is detoxifying thanks to its pectin content, contrasts arthritis and stimulates muscle function. It contains many minerals (above all potassium) and has a mild laxative effect.*
Oat *is rich in beta-glucan, a compound that reduces the absorption of cholesterol from foods, and trigonelline, an alkaloid that actively contrasts depression and has tonic effects. In addition, oat contains lectin, B-group vitamins and minerals such as calcium and phosphorus.*
Vanilla *is a sweet-smelling spice with an intense aroma. It is derived from a specific species of orchid.*

2 servings

2 apples
3/4 cup + 1 1/2 tbsp. (200 ml) soy milk
1 tsp. spice mix: cinnamon, pepper, nutmeg, clove

10 ice cubes
some cinnamon sticks and cloves for decoration

APPLE SMOOTHIE WITH SOY MILK AND SPICES

1. Wash the apples, peel them, remove the stem and core, cut into small pieces and place into the blender.

2. Add the spices, soy milk and ice. Blend until a smooth and homogeneous mixture is obtained.

3. Pour the beverage into glasses and decorated with cinnamon sticks and cloves.

4. *If you want to prepare soy milk, obtain 1/2 cup (100 grams) of yellow soybeans. Soak in 4 1/4 cups (1 liter) of water for about 20 hours then add another 2 cups (1/2 liter) of water and mix. Transfer the resulting mixture into 4 1/4 cups (1 liter) of boiling water and cook for 15 minutes. Allow to cool and filter through a strainer. Soy milk can be stored in the refrigerator for about 3 days.*

Difficulty: EASY
Preparation: **5 minutes**
Calories: **95 kcal**
per serving

Recipe Properties:

The Apple Smoothie with Soy Milk and Spices is an ideal blend for all individuals affected by circulatory diseases or diabetes, and who must lose weight. It is a very filling, highly hydrating and stimulating beverage.

Soybeans *lower cholesterol, control hunger and have positive effects on the metabolism.*
Apple *is a great resource for reducing "bad" cholesterol in the blood, which can lead to strokes and heart disease, due to its pectin contents. Because it also helps lower blood sugar levels, it is an excellent food for diabetics.*
Pepper, *one of the most common spices, is contained of water (about 10%), proteins, fats, and minerals including calcium, sodium, potassium, iron and phosphorus. Eating black pepper is not recommended to individuals with high blood pressure or hemorrhoids. In addition, it can interfere with some medicines.*

2 servings

1/3 cup (50 g) blueberries
1 pear

11/4 cups (300 ml) soy milk

BLUEBERRY SMOOTHIE WITH PEAR AND SOY MILK

1. Clean the blueberries. Wash them under running water and gently dry them with paper towels.

2. Peel the pear. Remove the stem and core, and cut into small pieces.

3. Place the soy milk, pieces of pear and blueberries into the blender jar. Blend until a smooth and homogeneous beverage is obtained.

4. For a blend that is thirst-quenching as well as nutritious, you can add ice to taste if the season permits. This beverage can make an excellent breakfast and is recommended to vegans or those interested in this dietary practice.

Difficulty: EASY
Preparation: **5 minutes**
Calories: **130 kcal**
per serving

Recipe Properties:
The Blueberry Smoothie with Pear and Soy Milk is a refreshing and hydrating beverage rich in antioxidants and fiber, which help prevent age-related illnesses. It supplies a good dose of vegetable proteins.

***Blueberry** is rich in hydrocinnamic acids, which can neutralize cancer-causing substances produced by the digestive system and slow down the process of ageing. It contains pterostilbene, a derivative of resvatrol (also present in red wine, grapes and in smaller amounts, in peanuts) that promotes weight loss making blueberries a perfect addition to low calorie diets.*
***Pear** helps keep energy levels up during heavy work.*
***Soybeans** contain isoflavones, which facilitate the function of sex hormones during menopause.*

2 servings

1 ripe pear
3/4 cup (200 ml) rice milk

1 scant cup (50 g) oat flakes

PEAR SMOOTHIE WITH RICE MILK AND OAT FLAKES

1. Wash the pear and peel it. Cut it into pieces allowing them to fall directly into the blender jar, and add the rice milk.

2. Blend until a homogeneous mixture is obtained. Pour it into glasses and serve with oat flakes.

3. This concoction is perfect for a balanced, nutritious, low-calorie breakfast. If you prefer a more velvety beverage, you can blend the oat flakes together with the other ingredients.

Difficulty: EASY
Preparation: **5 minutes**
Calories: **185 kcal**
per serving

Recipe Properties:
The Pear Smoothie with Rice Milk and Oat Flakes is highly energizing and great for replenishing energy after intense physical activity or psychophysical stress. It is very filling and due to its composition, provides a balanced supply of nutrients.

Rice milk is rich in calories and hence, important to individuals facing periods of extreme physical activity but is not recommended to diabetics. A good regulator of intestinal activity, it is suitable for those suffering from irritable bowl and excess stomach gases.
Pear contains minerals such as boron, potassium and magnesium, vitamins and fiber. It is a low calorie fruit with high water contents that help hydrate the body. It helps maintain energy levels high during prolonged physical activity.
Oat flakes are recommended for children and convalescents because of their considerable nutritive and invigorating properties. They contain a variety of anti-oxidant fatty acids including linoleic acid.

2 servings

1 organic pear
7 oz. (200 g) ripe mango

3/4 cup + 11/2 tbsp. (200 ml)
soy milk

PEAR SMOOTHIE WITH SOY MILK AND MANGO

1. Wash the pear. Remove the stem and core, cut into small pieces without removing the skin and place into the blender.

2. Wash the mango. Peel it and add to the pear.

3. Add the soy milk, blend and pour into glasses.

4. This nutritious and thirst-quenching smoothie takes on an almost hazelnut color given by the tannins contained in the skin of the pear. If you prefer the beverage to have the color of a mango (yellow), remove the skin for the pear and use only the pulp.

Difficulty: EASY
Preparation: **5 minutes**
Calories: **150 kcal**
per serving

Recipe Properties:
The Pear Smoothie with Soy Milk and Mango is a very filling beverage. Hence, it is useful in weight-loss diets. It is an ideal source of protein for individuals who don't like meat and beneficial to intestinal health.

Pear is recommended for prevention of cardiovascular diseases and for combatting high blood pressure. It has anti-tumor properties, aids in the elimination of intestinal slag and, due to its potassium contents, greatly helps prevent cramping.
Soy milk is an excellent source of proteins. According to some studies, it can help prevent tumors and some circulatory diseases.
Mango protects respiratory mucous membranes, tones the skin and promotes kidney function. In addition, it contains antioxidants and has depurative, diuretic and laxative properties.

1 serving　　7 oz. (200 g) ripe plum　　5 ice cubes (optional)
　　　　　　　1/2 cup (100 ml) oat milk

PLUM AND OAT MILK SMOOTHIE

1. Wash the plums, cut them into pieces, and remove the pits.

2. Pour the oat milk into the blender jar. Add the plums and the ice (if you want a thirst-quenching, refreshing beverage but the season precludes the use of ice, the smoothie is also great without it). Blend the ingredients until a smooth and homogeneous mixture is obtained.

3. Divide the smoothie among glasses and drink immediately.

4. *Oat milk can be prepared at home using 1 3/4 cups (100 grams) of oat flakes, 4 1/4 cups (1 liter) of water, 1 vanilla pod and 1 tablespoon of honey. Soak the oat flakes in water for 1 hour then filter and boil for 20 minutes with the vanilla pod. Finally, stir in the honey.*

Difficulty: EASY
Preparation: **5 minutes**
Calories: **96 kcal**

Recipe Properties:
The Plum and Oat Milk Smoothie is a laxative and detoxifying beverage that is rich in minerals, amino acids and antioxidant vitamins. It is excellent as a depurative, as an aid to weight-loss or for flushing the body of toxins.

Plum *is detoxifying and an excellent aid against constipation and stomachaches. The potassium it contains contrasts sodium and hence, reduces liquid retention in the tissues. Plum is rich in organic acids (which give it its mildly sour flavor), and helps balance the effects of a diet that is too rich in proteins.*
Oats *are a source of important fiber that helps regularize intestinal transit and reduce the absorption of cholesterol. They are rich in essential amino acids such as lysine, which is present in small quantities in other cereals.*

1 serving

1/4 cup (50 ml) cherry syrup
1/2 cup (100 ml) rice milk
5 ice cubes

10 syruped cherries
1 wood skewer

CHERRY SYRUP AND RICE MILK SMOOTHIE

1. To prepare a syrup with no added sugar, simmer ripe, pitted fruit over low heat until a soft puree is obtained. Once cooled, the mixture must be blended and filtered. At this point, they syrup is ready for use.

2. Pour the cherry syrup, rice milk and ice into the blender jar.

3. Prepare a skewer of syruped cherries. Blend the ingredients until a homogeneous beverage is obtained.

4. Divide among glasses and add the skewer.

5. The smoothie is ready to be drunk or stored in the refrigerator.

Difficulty: EASY
Preparation: **5 minutes**
Calories: **140 kcal**

Recipe Properties:

The Cherry Syrup and Rice Milk Smoothie is depurative, mildly laxative and rich in antioxidants. When making this beverage, it is fundamental to use syrup prepared at home or originating from a well-known company in order to avoid the ingestion of useless and toxic additives and preservatives.

Cherry is a great aid to flushing the body of toxins; it is mildly laxative, depurative and beneficial to the liver. It has anti-inflammatory and painkilling properties due to the presence of numerous anthocianosides. It is rich in soluble fiber, which gives a sense of fullness. In addition, it contains melatonin, a compound useful to cardiac health and fundamental for combatting insomnia.
Rice milk contains antioxidant unsaturated fats, minerals and large amounts of simple sugars. It is an important resource for individuals performing intense physical activity because it is very energizing; it is a good regulator of intestinal function and beneficial to irritable colon sufferers.

1 serving

1/3 cup (50 g) blackberries
1/3 cup (50 g) raspberries
1/3 cup (100 g) soy yogurt

Difficulty: EASY
Preparation: **10 minutes**
Calories: **100 kcal**

SOY YOGURT SMOOTHIE WITH RASPBERRY AND BLACKBERRY JUICES

1. Clean the wild berries, wash them under running water and leave to dry on paper towels.

2. Place some blackberries and raspberries aside to use for decoration. Juice the rest of the fruit in a centrifugal juicer and catch the juice into a glass. This step allows to eliminate the seeds present in the berries obtaining in this way a smooth mixture (if you don't have a centrifugal juicer, you can filter the mixture through a strainer).

3. Blend 2/3 of the yogurt with the juice. Pour into a glass leaving a small amount of the smoothie in the blender jar. Top with the remaining yogurt and finally, with the rest of the smoothie.

4. Decorate with the blackberries and raspberries and enjoy immediately this magnificent smoothie, which can be transformed into an irresistible sorbet.

Raspberry is excellent for blood circulation and cleansing, and helps digestion.
Blackberry protects circulation. It is rich in vitamins A, B9 and C, and acids such as citric, malic and tartaric acids, all of which are useful in weight-loss diets. It contains fiber and minerals such as potassium, copper, calcium and manganese as well as many antioxidants such as flavonoids and anthocianosides, which actively combat degenerative diseases.
Soy yogurt is an important depurative and an aid to weight-loss diets.

Recipe Properties:

The Soy Yogurt Smoothie with Raspberry and Blackberry Juices is a beverage that helps fight the cold, replenishes energy and fortifies the immune system. It is a highly stimulating beverage with a pleasant flavor and irresistible color.

1 serving

3 1/2 oz. (100 g) pear
1/3 cup (100 g) soy yogurt
1/3 cup (50 g) mixed wild
berries
3 1/2 oz. (100 g) pineapple
wood skewers

Difficulty: EASY
Preparation: **15 minutes**
Calories: **170 kcal**

SOY YOGURT SMOOTHIE WITH PEAR, PINEAPPLE AND WILD BERRY JUICE

1. Peel the pear. Cut it into small pieces (set two or three aside) and blend them with the yogurt.

2. Clean, gently wash and leave the wild berries to dry on paper towels.

3. Peel the pineapple and cut it into pieces. Prepare the pear and pineapple skewers and place them on a saucer.

4. Pour the smoothie into glasses, decorate with the fruit and enjoy this refreshing and flavorful snack immediately.

5. This smoothie is perfect as a refreshing breakfast or end to a meal.

Soybeans play and important role in the protection against some forms of cancer.
Pineapple is rich in vitamins A, C and B-group vitamins, and has a good amount of minerals, particularly potassium and manganese.
Raspberry and **blueberry** are wild berries that are detoxifying, slimming and rich in anthocianosides. They protect against degenerative diseases.
Pear is very rich in fiber and extremely helpful in regularizing intestinal transit.

Recipe Properties:
The Soy Yogurt Smoothie with Pear, Pineapple and Wild Berry Juice has a very pleasant flavor and intense aroma. It is highly hydrating, beneficial to the immune system and fortifies our defenses against cold season illnesses.

2 servings

11/2 cups (200 g) strawberries
2 ripe figs
3/4 cup (200 g) soy yogurt

2 tbsp. (20 g) toasted and
chopped hazelnuts (or crushed
hazelnuts)

SOY YOGURT, STRAWBERRY SYRUP AND CRUSHED HAZELNUT SMOOTHIE

1. Clean the strawberries, rinse them under running water, remove the stems and set 2 aside to use for decoration.

2. Cut the strawberries into small pieces and place into a pot. Peel the figs and add them to the strawberries. Cook until the fruit has disintegrated and reduced in volume. Allow to cool and filter.

3. Place back over heat and continue to cook until the syrup volume is reduced by half (this way, you will have a syrup with no added sugar).

4. When it is time to serve, blend half of the cooled syrup with the yogurt and half of the chopped hazelnuts. Pour into glasses, top with some syrup and left over chopped hazelnuts, and decorate with the strawberries.

5. This smoothie is an excellent, satisfying snack or well-worth dessert. It can be prepared in advance or transformed into an ice cream.

Difficulty: MEDIUM
Preparation: **40 minutes**
Calories: **170 kcal**
per serving

Recipe Properties:

The Soy Yogurt, Strawberry Syrup and Crushed Hazelnut Smoothie is very filling, suitable for weight-loss diets, rich in active constituents, minerals and vitamins. It is helpful in the prevention of infective and degenerative diseases.

Strawberry *facilitates intestinal transit, regularizes cholesterol levels in the blood and combats bad breath.*
Soybeans *are a plant with the absolute highest amount of protein.*
Hazelnut *is rich in unsaturated Omega 3 fatty acids, although not as rich as walnut. It contains phytosterols, which aid proper cardiac and circulatory function, and, after almonds, it is the nut with the greatest amount of antioxidant vitamin E. Regular assumption of hazelnut can reduce LDL ("bad" cholesterol) and triglyceride levels in the blood.*

2 servings

4 fresh chili peppers,
   Holland or similar (mild)
4 small, fresh or dried
   chili peppers
   (moderately spicy)
3/4 cup + 1 1/2 tbsp.
   (200 ml) soy milk
salt (optional)

Difficulty: EASY
Preparation: **5 minutes**
Calories: **65 kcal**
per serving

SPICY CHILI PEPPER AND SOY MILK SMOOTHIE

1. Wash the Holland chili peppers, remove the stems, seeds and white portions then cut into pieces and place into the blender jar. Set aside the other chili peppers, which will serve to decorate the smoothie.

2. Add the soy milk and if you like, a pinch of salt.

3. Briefly blend until the ingredients are well amalgamated producing an appealing pastel-colored beverage.

4. Pour into glasses, decorate with the remaining chili peppers, brake into pieces for spice lovers, and serve.

5. This smoothie is a stimulating and appetizing burst of flavor and makes an excellent aperitif. It can be stored in the refrigerator for a few hours before drinking.

Soybeans contain many of the essential amino acids. In addition, they are one of the few protein-rich foods that can help elevate the percentage of high-density cholesterol (HDL or "good" cholesterol), which helps protect the arteries.
Chili pepper contains antioxidant bioflavonoids, great amounts of vitamin C and capsaicin, a compound thought to help prevent prostate cancer. In addition, it can improve digestion and benefit circulation.

Recipe Properties:
The Spicy Chili Pepper and Soy Milk Smoothie is a very stimulating beverage particularly suitable to hot climates. It is slimming, favors proper function of the metabolism and provides a rich supply of amino acids and antioxidants that protect from intestinal infections.

170

2 servings

4 prickly pears
3/4 cup + 11/2 tbsp. (200
  ml) almond milk
6 almonds

Difficulty: MEDIUM
Preparation: **10 minutes**
Calories: **145 kcal**
per serving

PRICKLY PEAR JUICE
WITH ALMOND MILK

1. Wash the prickly pears wearing gloves, to avoid being pricked by the micro spines covering the fruit. Make a length-wise cut into the skin, roll the skin off and juice 2 of the pears in a centrifugal juicer.

2. Place the almond milk, almonds, prickly pear juice and the 2 remaining pears into the blender jar. Blend until a smooth mixture is obtained.

3. If you prefer a beverage free of prickly pear seeds, filter the mixture through a strainer before drinking.

4. Divide among glasses and serve immediately.

Prickly pear is extremely rich in water and in glucose, fructose, and pectin. It has many minerals, particularly potassium, phosphorus, calcium and magnesium, and vitamin C. It has laxative properties and its consumption is not recommended to diabetics. Different contents of antioxidant anthocyanins in the fruit determine the color of the prickly pear, which is characteristic for its variety of tones: green, orange, yellow, bright red.
Almond milk contains vitamin E, fiber, minerals such as calcium, magnesium, selenium, iron, manganese, potassium and phosphorus, and unsaturated fatty acids including oleic acid. It can be used in weight-loss diets because it is very filling. It has thirst-quenching, refreshing, anti-depressant and anti-inflammatory properties.

Recipe Properties:
The Prickly Pear Juice with Almond Milk is energizing, excellent for combatting cold season illnesses, and rich in substances that help fight age-related and free radical triggered diseases.

JUICES, EMULSIONS AND SMOOTHIES WITH ANIMAL PROTEINS

A TREASURE CHEST OF TASTE AND FLAVOR

by Cinzia Trenchi

There is no denying that smoothies and milkshakes are traditionally prepared with cow milk. At least one refreshing, delicious and creamy blend of fruit that is inviting and aromatic is almost certain to be among our memories. A blend that recreates moments of pure pleasure: a cuddle for the palate to enjoy through a straw, in great gulps or in spoonfuls. In this section, dedicated to the tradition of milk, ricotta and yogurt-based blends, intriguing suggestions for pairing vegetables (cucumbers, for example) and spices with yogurt, milk with dates, and ricotta with dried fruit and nuts, are proposed. These should be included in the diet in moderation because they are naturally richer in calories compared to beverages from the previous sections. Smoothies with animal proteins are intended above all for children or for moments when time is short but the need for a good dose of energy is great, such as before physical activity or on a morning of studying or work. When choosing between sweet and savory, the only thing that counts is personal preference for the flavors involved. Of course, for children, it is best to choose fruit. However, for an adult palate there are combinations – such as eggs and spinach, or yogurt, cucumber and spices – that will prove extremely satisfying and will help break up the monotony of flavors. These beverages are also ideal for blocking sudden hunger pangs and getting a boost of energy, without infringing the rules of a healthy diet. They are extremely simple and quick to prepare: a concentrate of flavor highlighted by a touch of the exotic, like vanilla, toasted seeds, nuts and dried fruit: all flavors that readily blend together, exalting one another in the process. Some preparations in this section, such as those with nuts, dried fruit and spices, can be stored in the refrigerator without the flavor being affected. The same is true for vanilla milk, which once boiled with vanilla beans and filtered, can stay in the refrigerator for a couple of days.

ENERGIZING COMBINATIONS

by Maurizio Cusani

*A*nimal proteins contained in foods such as cow milk, yogurt and egg yolk are the most energizing and filling foods of all. This explains the existence of egg, milk and yogurt weight-loss mono-diets. These foods are low in sugars but capable of satisfying the sense of hunger by triggering the secretion of compounds such as cholecystokinin.

Animal proteins provide an enormous charge and are recommended at any point during an illness. In addition, they do not contain too many nitrogenous compounds, unlike white and red meat, but do contain noble proteins, which are rich in all the essential amino acids. Hence, they are capable of quickly repairing damaged tissues. Furthermore, they do not overload the pancreas by infringing sugar metabolism and are suitable to individuals prone to diabetes. Finally, these proteins are easier to digest with respect to those in meat and have a combination of nutrients that is particularly useful for getting healthy, especially when mixed with fruit and vegetables. They also contain unsaturated fatty acids and lectin, which keep the arteries clean, and a wide range of minerals and vitamins, particularly B-group vitamins.

In short, even animal proteins, if properly balanced with vegetable proteins, can help us lose weight and benefit our health in any season and at any age. And let's not forget, they are a treasure chest of flavors.

1 serving

2 1/3 tbsp. (20 g) toasted and
salted pistachios
1/4 cup (50 g) ricotta

1/2 cup (100 g) low fat milk
freshly ground pepper

PISTACHIO EMULSION WITH RICOTTA AND MILK

1. Shell the pistachios. Place them into the blender jar with the ricotta, season with pepper to taste and add the milk.

2. Emulsify the ingredients until a velvety, soft and creamy mixture is obtained.

3. Transfer into a glass or a bowl and enjoy with fresh vegetables or on its own, as you prefer.

4. This emulsion is an exceptional snack that is rich in flavor, appetizing and lends itself well to being served as an appetizer or an aperitif!

Difficulty: EASY
Preparation: **7 minutes**
Calories: **170 kcal**

Recipe Properties:
The Pistachio Emulsion with Ricotta and Milk is an energizing, filling, hydrating and slimming beverage that can prevent metabolic disorders and age-related diseases, especially those related to circulation.

Ricotta inhibits the development of diabetes and, if included in a low-calorie diet, helps reduce obesity.
Pistachio is anti-inflammatory and contributes to lowering low-density cholesterol (LDL, or "bad" cholesterol), which can damage the arteries. It contains polyphenols with antioxidant properties, vitamin A, iron and phosphorus. For this reason, it is considered a restorative to the nervous system. Its isoflavones can strengthen the immune system. Unsalted, it also lowers blood pressure and improves digestion.
Milk is a good regulator of intestinal function but is not very suitable for individuals with irritable bowels or colitis.

2 servings

1/4 cup (50 g) sheep's milk
 ricotta
3/4 cups + 1 1/2 tbsp. (200 ml)
 low fat cow milk

1/4 cup (50 g) dried, pitted dates
10 ice cubes (optional)

SMOOTHIE WITH DATES, MILK AND RICOTTA

1. Place the ricotta, milk and dates into the blender.

2. Blend the ingredients until a soft and creamy mixture is obtained. The smoothie will naturally tend to separate, with the dates floating to the top and the more fluid portion sinking to the bottom. It can be stored in the refrigerator for a few hours, but only if it is prepared without the ice.

3. This magnificent, energetic and satisfying beverage becomes thirst-quenching if diluted with some ice. Its flavor is dominated by the creaminess and natural sweetness of the date..

Difficulty: EASY
Preparation: **5 minutes**
Calories: **130 kcal**
per serving

Recipe Properties:

The Smoothie with Dates, Milk and Ricotta is very filling, rich in noble proteins and helps protect gastrointestinal organs. Highly energizing, it is recommended to individuals who need to quickly regain energy after intense physical or mental activity.

Date is rich in iron, magnesium and potassium, vitamin C and B-group vitamins, fiber and many sugars, which make it highly energizing. It is useful for lowering "bad" cholesterol (LDL) but not recommended to diabetics. Despite being low in calories, it is filling.
Milk protects the large intestine from tumor growth, adequately hydrates the body due to its high water content and improves concentration.
Ricotta, being just a dairy product, has substantially lower cholesterol and fat contents than cheese.

2 servings

3/4 cups + 1 1/2 tbsp.
  (200 ml) low fat cow milk
1 yellow peach
1/4 cup (50 g) chopped
  Cantaloupe melon
1/3 cup (50 g) strawberries
1/3 cup (50 g) blackberries

Difficulty: EASY
Preparation: **12 minutes**
Calories: **80 kcal**
per serving

SMOOTHIE WITH PEACH, STRAWBERRIES, MELON, BLACKBERRIES AND MILK

1. Peel the peach, remove the pit, cut into pieces and place into a bowl. Wash the strawberries under running water, remove the stems, cut into 2 or 4 pieces depending on their size and add to the peach.

2. Gently wash the blackberries under running water and add them and the melon to the peach.

3. Transfer the fruit into the blender jar, add the milk and blend the ingredients until a homogeneous mixture is obtained.

4. It is an excellent light breakfast. It is possible to render the smoothie even more thirst-quenching by adding ice during preparation.

Strawberry *is an excellent addition to any weight-loss diet.*
Peach *contains potassium, iron, calcium, phosphorus, sodium and fiber. It is rich in vitamin A but above all in vitamins C, E and K. This fruit greatly helps to keep skin healthy and prevents gastrointestinal disorders.*
Cantaloupe melon *is rich in water, mildly laxative, hydrating and refreshing. It is rich in iron, calcium, phosphorus, potassium, fiber and vitamins (A, C, B-group).*
Milk *is the most nutritionally complete food for growing children. It has high contents of calcium, phosphorus, potassium and magnesium.*

Recipe Properties:
The Smoothie with Peach, Strawberries, Melon, Blackberries and Milk is a beverage that has depura- tive and detoxifying actions, and a very pleasant flavor. Energizing and filling, it helps regulate the digestive system and the intestinal tract, and is recommended also for children.

2 servings

1 coconut
1/4 cup (50 g) low fat
yogurt
1 banana

Difficulty: DIFFICULT
Preparation: **15 minutes**
Calories: **160 kcal**
per serving

BANANA, COCONUT MILK AND YOGURT SMOOTHIE

1. Pierce the base of the coconut (the softest part of the nut) with a bodkin and catch the milk into a glass.

2. Open the shell using a hard object. When opening the coconut, try to keep the two halves of the shell intact so they can be used as bowls.

3. Blend the yogurt with the banana, coconut milk and the equivalent of one tablespoon of coconut pulp until a homogeneous and smooth mixture is obtained.

4. Divide among glasses or bowls and serve immediately.

Banana has antidepressant properties and is rich in carbohydrates and minerals (potassium, magnesium), which are fundamental to sports enthusiasts.
Yogurt (a term of Turkish origins) is a very old food. Nutritious, detoxifying, low in calories, easily digestible and depurative, it is great for the elderly, children and pregnant women.
Coconut milk is a greatly valued dietary supplement. It is depurative, filling and a valid aid against high blood pressure, stress and cellulite. It strengthens the immune system and contains vitamins and numerous minerals including potassium, which is present in large amounts.

Recipe Properties:
The Banana, Coconut Milk and Yogurt Smoothie is a suitable substitute for a full meal and an excellent aid in diets. In addition to being energizing, it has a very high satiety index.

179

1 serving

1 celery heart
3 1/2 oz. (100 g) baked beet
1/3 cup (100 g) low fat yogurt

1 tbsp. lemon juice
salt and 1 pinch chili pepper
2 wooden skewers

BEET, YOGURT AND CELERY SMOOTHIE

1. Clean and wash the celery. Take two celery sticks, break them into pieces and place into the blender jar.

2. Remove the external skin from the beets (if present) and add 2/3 of the pulp in pieces to the blender jar (keep the remainder for making skewers, which will add color to the smoothie).

3. Prepare the skewers using 1 or 2 celery sticks and the remaining beets.

4. Season the ingredients in the blender with salt, chili pepper, and lemon juice, and add the yogurt.

5. Blend until a creamy and homogeneous mixture is obtained. Pour it into a glass and add some flavor with the celery heart and the skewers.

6. An excellent snack and a satisfying treat, it can also serve as a pleasant appetizer that is both flavorful and low in calories!

Difficulty: EASY
Preparation: **10 minutes**
Calories: **71 kcal**

Recipe Properties:
The Beet, Yogurt and Celery Smoothie is a depurative and filling beverage with many properties beneficial in the prevention of age-related diseases of the nervous and immune systems.

Beet is an ideal food for weakness and anemia sufferers because it stimulates the production of red blood cells. It also protects the liver, improves physical performance and regulates arterial pressure.
Glutamic acid contained in beets promotes the proper function of the nervous system.
Yogurt has acidulous characteristics due to the presence of milk enzymes, which transform lactose into lactic acid making it easy to digest even by individuals incapable of producing lactase.
Celery has a depurative and diuretic effect and is a natural stimulant due to its aspartic acid contents.

1 serving

1 cucumber
1/3 cup (100 g) dense yogurt
(Greek or similar)

1 tbsp. spice mix composed of:
turmeric, chili pepper, pepper,
cumin, coriander
salt (optional)

CUCUMBER AND YOGURT SMOOTHIE WITH SPICES AND SALT

1. Wash the cucumber, peel it, cut it into pieces and place into the blender jar with 2 tablespoons of yogurt. If the cucumber is ripe, you can blend it without adding the yogurt because it is an extremely water-rich vegetable.

2. Pour the smoothie into a bowl, add the remaining yogurt and manually blend the mixture using a whisk until a homogeneous beverage is obtained.

3. Transfer into a glass, season with spices to taste and flavor with salt.

4. This very tasty preparation is great as a refreshing and light summer snack, and perfect as a dip for chopped vegetables.

Difficulty: EASY
Preparation: **5 minutes**
Calories: **94 kcal**

Recipe Properties:
The Cucumber and Yogurt Smoothie with Spices and Salt is a filling beverage with an unusual but pleasant flavor that speeds up the metabolism and hence, aids in flushing and weight-loss treatments.

Cucumber contains a large amount of water (equal to 90%) and tartaric acid, which is very helpful in weight-loss. This vegetable helps reduce water retention and swollen eyelids (by applying fresh pulp to the eye), and fights cellulite and stretch marks. In addition, it reduces the symptoms of fibromyalgia and chronic fatigue syndrome.
Turmeric is rich in a particularly efficient antioxidant compound: curcumin.
Chili pepper is naturally slimming because it acts directly on the nervous system reducing the sense of hunger and stimulates the metabolism helping to burn fats. It can aid in the regulation of carbohydrate metabolism and has pain-reducing and anti-inflammatory properties.
Yogurt contains many B-group vitamins and is easier to digest than milk.

2 servings

1 1/4 cups (300 ml) whole cow
  milk
3 1/2 oz. (100 g) pineapple
1 lime

2 passion fruit
1 tbsp. coconut pulp
1 vanilla pod

VANILLA MILK SMOOTHIE WITH TROPICAL FRUIT

1. First, prepare vanilla milk by boiling milk with a vanilla pod for about 5 minutes, filtering it through a sieve and allowing it to cool. Milk thus flavored can be stored in the refrigerator for a few days.

2. Wash the fruit, peel the pineapple and juice the lime. Cut open the passion fruit and extract the pulp.

3. Cut all of the fruit into pieces and place them into the blender jar. Add the lime juice and the milk, and blend until a homogeneous mixture is obtained.

4. Divide among glasses and drink immediately to fully enjoy the aromas and complex flavor of this preparation.

Difficulty: MEDIUM
Preparation: **15 minutes**
Calories: **160 kcal**
per serving

Recipe Properties:
The Vanilla Milk Smoothie with Tropical Fruit has an extremely pleasant and aromatic flavor and is very rich in vitamins, minerals and antioxidants. It is a good stimulant for the nervous system and combats age-related diseases.

__Coconut__ combats air swallowing, stimulates the immune system and promotes ossification. It also stimulates the central nervous system and improves concentration. The interior of the coconut contains water that is perfectly potable (a coconut is made up of 50% water).
__Passion fruit__ aids against gastritis, colitis and water retention, and is an anti-inflammatory.
__Vanilla__ has antidepressant properties and supplies an irresistible aroma.
__Pineapple__ can be validly used to treat swelling, cellulite, muscle trauma and venous insufficiency.

2 servings   7 oz. (200 g) Cantaloupe melon   1/3 cup (100 g) low fat cow milk
1 orange   yogurt

CANTALOUPE MELON, ORANGE JUICE AND YOGURT SMOOTHIE

1. Wash the melon, remove the skin, the seeds and the fibrous portions, and cut into pieces.

2. Juice the orange and pour the juice into the blender jar. Add the yogurt and the melon, and blend until a homogeneous mixture is obtained.

3. Divide among glasses and drink immediately to enjoy this smoothie's magnificent flavor.

4. Delicious and thirst-quenching: these are the words that come to mind while tasting this amazing beverage, which should be consumed for breakfast or as a snack. If you want to make it even more thirst-quenching and if the season permits, you can dilute it with some ice.

Difficulty: EASY
Preparation: **10 minutes**
Calories: **133 kcal**
per serving

Recipe Properties:
The Cantaloupe Melon, Orange Juice and Yogurt Smoothie is a highly balanced beverage with antioxidant and protective properties that is filling and suitable to any diet. In addition, it improves concentration and provides an important support to mental activity.

Cantaloupe melon *is a variety of summer melon with a smooth skin and dark green stripes. It has a penetrating aroma and delicious orange pulp. It is rich in beta-carotene, a substance also contained in carrots that gives it its orange color and is transformed by the body into vitamin A. Because it is low in calories, it is recommended for all diets.*
Orange *is recommended for controling blood pressure and preventing heart diseases.*
Yogurt *is an easily digestible food: it is assimilated by the body in about one hour!*

1 serving

1 orange
13/4 oz. (50 g) green
  apples
3 tbsp. (20 g) dried
  cranberries
1/4 cup (50 g) sheep's milk
  ricotta

Difficulty: EASY
Preparation: **6 minutes**
Calories: **130 kcal**

RICOTTA, APPLE, ORANGE AND DRIED CRANBERRY SMOOTHIE

1. Juice the orange. Filter the juice and pour it into the blender.

2. Peel the apple. Cut it into small pieces and add to the orange juice together with the cranberries and the ricotta.

3. Briefly blend until a homogeneous cream is obtained, pour into glasses and drink this excellent smoothie immediately.

4. Easy and fast to prepare, it is a tasty snack with a balanced flavor perfect as an energetic and well-rounded breakfast.

Recipe Properties:

The Ricotta, Apple, Orange and Dried Cranberry Smoothie is hydrating, thirst-quenching and rich in antioxidant and circulation-protecting substances. It is very filling, improves the equilibrium of the immune and gastrointestinal systems, and has a flavor that children love.

Sheep's milk ricotta *supplies a large amount of highly nutritious proteins and calcium, which contributes to bone health and effectively blocks hunger.*
Apple *contains many vitamins and Omega 3 fatty acids, helpful in combatting the symptoms of asthma.*
Orange *is very useful in regaining energy during convalescence, intense physical activity or cold season illnesses.*
Cranberry *is rich in minerals and vitamin C. It promotes intestinal flora and strengthens the immune system due to its antioxidant content.*

2 servings

1 cup (200 g) baby
  spinach
2 tbsp. cooking cream
1 tbsp. lemon juice
1 tbsp. extra virgin
  olive oil
2 egg yolks
salt and pepper

Difficulty: MEDIUM
Preparation: **10 minutes**
Calories: **140 kcal**
per serving

SPINACH AND EGG YOLK SMOOTHIE WITH LEMON AND PEPPER

1. Clean the spinach in a cold-water bath. Rinse it several times to remove any traces of earth from the leaves and drain.

2. Extract the juice from half of the spinach in a centrifugal juicer, catch the juice and pour it into the blender jar.

3. Add the cream, remaining spinach and olive oil. Blend until a smooth a creamy mixture is obtained. Divide between two small cups or bowls, top with an egg yolk and season with a few drops of lemon juice, salt and pepper.

4. Recommended for an energizing breakfast, it is also perfect as an original and intriguing appetizer!

Lemon is an ideal fruit for combatting loss of energy, exhaustion and cold-triggered arthritis pain.
Pepper is diuretic, promotes weight-loss and digestion, and has beneficial effects on the metabolism. It comes in many varieties: white, green, pink and black (the most common). It is not recommended for those suffering from high blood pressure or hemorrhoids.
Spinach contains a lot of vitamin C and folic acid. Its consumption is important for sufferers of allergies, anemia, dermatitis or endocrine disorders.
Egg yolk has an elevated amount of vitamins and minerals.

Proprietà della ricetta:
The Spinach and Egg Yolk Smoothie with Lemon and Pepper is very filling, energizing and can readily substitute a complete meal. It stimulates the metabolism burning calories dangerous to health, aids microcirculation and is rich in vitamin C.

2 servings

2/3 cup (100 g) grapes
1 apple

1 pear
1/3 cup (100 g) low fat yogurt

GRAPE, PEAR AND APPLE SMOOTHIE WITH YOGURT

1. Wash the grapes, apple and pear. Peel the apple and the pear, remove the stems and the cores, and cut into small pieces. Detach the grape berries from the stalk, cut them into halves and remove the seeds.

2. Place the yogurt, grapes, and pieces of the apple and pear into the blender jar.

3. Blend until a homogeneous mixture is obtained, pour it into glasses and serve immediately.

4. This smoothie is an excellent extremely thirst-quenching breakfast with a satisfying flavor. It can be diluted with ice to render it even more thirst-quenching or transformed into a sorbet by churning in an ice cream maker for 30 minutes.

Difficulty: EASY
Preparation: **12 minutes**
Calories: **133 kcal**
per serving

Recipe Properties:

The Grape, Pear and Apple Smoothie with Yogurt is very filling, excellent for regularizing intestinal transit and recommended as protection against all cold season illnesses. In addition, it is highly detoxifying for smokers and individuals living in cities plagued by smog.

Grapes *are a fruit composed of numerous small berries rich in easily digestible and absorbable simple sugars, such as glucose and fructose. They also contain B-group vitamins, particularly B1, B2 and PP, vitamins A and C, minerals and antioxidants such as resvartrol.*
Apple *seems to have a detoxifying effect on the body, particularly in smokers.*
Pear *acts in harmony with the fiber contained in the apples, while also exalting the properties of the pectin.*
Yogurt *contains lactose, which is broken down into two other sugars (glucose and galactose), which don't trigger any intolerances in individuals who consume this food.*

2 servings

4 pitted dried apricots (about 1/3 cup, 40 g)

6 pitted prunes (about 1/4 cup, 50 g)

2/3 cup (200 g) dense low fat yogurt

2 plums and 2 apricots for decoration

YOGURT SMOOTHIE WITH PRUNES AND DRIED APRICOTS

1. Cut the dried fruit into small pieces and place into the blender jar together with the yogurt. Turn on the appliance and blend until a dense, homogeneous and creamy mixture is obtained.

2. Pour the smoothie into glasses, decorate with prunes and dried apricots and serve.

3. It is a smoothie that can be stored in the refrigerator for a few hours with no change in flavor. It can also be transformed into an excellent dessert by churning in the ice cream maker for 30 minutes.

Difficulty: EASY
Preparation: **6 minutes**
Calories: **130 kcal per serving**

Recipe Properties:

The Yogurt Smoothie with Prunes and Dried Apricots is a beverage that is almost as rich and filling as a meal. It is easy to digest and great for individuals who suffer from constipation or need a quick energy boost after intense physical activity or psycho-physical stress.

Yogurt *is milk coagulated by specific bacteria. It is very rich in calcium, easy to digest because it contains just 3% lactose, and can even be consumed by lactose-intolerant individuals.*

Plum *has strong laxative properties due to its contents of dyphenil isatin. It contains antioxidant, anti-degenerative and tonic substances such as quercitin, stimulates bile secretion and promotes digestion.*

Dried apricot *conserves all the minerals present in the fresh fruit and is very rich in fiber, which promotes proper intestinal function.*

2 servings

3 tbsp. (50 g) mixed flower honey
3/4 cup (200 g) goat milk yogurt

1 pinch of ground cinnamon
2 small pieces of a cinnamon stick

YOGURT AND HONEY SMOOTHIE WITH CINNAMON

1. In a bowl, blend 2/3 of the honey, the yogurt and the cinnamon powder with an electric mixer. Pour the mixture into two cups.

2. Use the remaining honey to decorate the top of the mixture by drizzling it from a spoon and add aroma with a piece of a cinnamon stick.

3. This is a very simple preparation with an excellent flavor and delightful aroma: as simple as it is delicious. In addition, honey, when consumed in moderate amounts, is an excellent sweetener that is nutritious and calorie-rich. Overall, it contained 303 kcal per every 1/3 cup (100 grams)!

Difficulty: EASY
Preparation: **5 minutes**
Calories: **135 kcal**
per serving

Recipe Properties:
The Yogurt and Honey Smoothie with Cinnamon is a very pleasant and aromatic beverage that is filling, very energizing, and ideal after psychophysical stress or during convalescence. It is hydrating, promotes digestion and is recommended to individuals with intestinal disorders.

Goat milk yogurt is very easy to digest and can strengthen the immune system.
Honey is a compound that has been pre-digested by bees and is therefore very easily assimilated by the body. It is a treasure chest of energy.
Cinnamon is a spice with significant antioxidant properties. It contains numerous tannins and camphor. It is antiseptic, anti-bacterial, and antispasmodic, due to its trypsin contents, facilitates the digestion of blood lipids and regularizes blood sugar levels. Cinnamon also combats intestinal fermentation and decreases the appetite. Recently, it has also been hypothesized to have a positive effect on neurologic diseases and dementia.

1 serving

1 medium zucchini
2 tbsp. cooking cream
1 egg yolk

1 tsp. (about 5 g) seed mix: white
   and black sesame and garden
   cress
salt and pepper

ZUCCHINI AND EGG YOLK SMOOTHIE WITH SESAME SEEDS AND GARDEN CRESS

1. Toast the seeds separately in a non-stick frying pan to render them tastier and easier to digest.

2. Wash the zucchini, trim the ends, cut into pieces and place into the blender.

3. Blend the zucchini with the cream and once a soft and homogeneous mixture is obtained, transfer it onto a bowl. Season with salt and pepper to taste, add the egg yolk and mix.

Difficulty: MEDIUM
Preparation: **10 minutes**
Calories: **156 kcal**

4. Pour the blend into a glass, flavor with toasted seeds and enjoy this beverage with its winning flavor and crunchy yet creamy consistency.

Recipe Properties:
The Zucchini and Egg Yolk Smoothie with Sesame Seeds and Garden Cress is a very filling beverage that can replace a meal. It is rich in substances that protect the body from age-related diseases, and favors intestinal transit and circulation.

Zucchini *is an easily digestible vegetable that is rich in water (in amounts equal to 94% of its weight) and low in calories.*
Egg yolk *contains a lot of lactin. Lactin stimulates high-density cholesterol (HDL or "good" cholesterol), which keeps blood vessels elastic and healthy and improves circulation.*
Garden cress *contains a lot of minerals, particularly iron and in smaller amounts, manganese, copper, zinc, phosphorus, iodine and calcium. In addition, it has high concentrations of vitamins B2, A, PP, A and above all, C.*
Sesame seeds *are rich in calcium, zinc, phosphorus, selenium, potassium, copper and magnesium. Their consumption helps to keep the immune system healthy and to recover strength after great excretion or illness.*

2 servings

1 cucumber
1 zucchini
1/3 cup (100 g) low fat yogurt

1 tbsp. lemon juice
salt and pepper

ZUCCHINI, CUCUMBER AND YOGURT SMOOTHIE

1. Wash the cucumber, trim the ends and set aside a few slices to use for decoration. Peel the rest of the vegetable, cut into pieces and place into the blender jar.

2. Wash the zucchini, trim the ends, slice and add to the cucumber.

3. Add the yogurt, and finish with pepper and salt to taste, and lemon juice. Blend until a smooth and creamy mixture is obtained.

4. Pour into glasses, decorate with slices of cucumber and serve immediately.

5. In addition to being a refreshing beverage or a pleasant, extremely low-fat snack, this smoothie can also be used as a dressing for salads.

Difficulty: EASY
Preparation: **7 minutes**
Calories: **42 kcal**
per serving

Recipe Properties:
The Zucchini, Cucumber and Yogurt Smoothie is a very thirst-quenching and diuretic beverage that is beneficial to the gastrointestinal system and an ideal defense against degenerative, vascular and eye diseases, and cancer.

Zucchini is a vegetable that is rich in antioxidants, such as the xanthines, which have anti-degenerative properties.
Cucumber is a vegetable that has diuretic and detoxifying properties. It contains mucilage and phytosterols, which lower cholesterol and seem to have anti-tumor properties as well.
Yogurt, in addition to the benefits of the milk proteins it contains, which are required for child growth, contains B-group vitamins. Milk enzymes composing it are fundamental for keeping the digestive system healthy and whole. In addition, it protects the gastrointestinal system, particularly during treatment with antibiotics.

**one quart (one liter)
of milk**

4 1/4 cups (1 liter) whole milk   4 vanilla pods

VANILLA MILK

1. Vanilla milk is an aromatic and delicious base that can be used in numerous preparations and can be stored in the refrigerator for a few days.

2. Break the vanilla beans and add to the milk. Boil over low heat for 5 minutes.

3. Allow to cool then filter through a strainer.

4. Vanilla milk is delicious even on its own, at room temperature, but can also be transformed into a refreshing and thirst-quenching beverage by the addition of a few ice cubes.

Difficulty: EASY
Preparation: **7 minutes**
Calories: **63 kcal per dl**

Recipe Properties:
Vanilla Milk is very energizing and suitable for regaining strength after intense physical activity and during convalescence. It has a pleasant aroma and because it fills up the stomach, gives a sense of fullness that is very useful in weight-loss diets.

Milk can prove difficult to digest by adults with low levels of lactase. Lactase will continue to be produced by the body if milk is consumed continuously from childhood. Milk, which is rich in calcium, is beneficial to dentition and ossification, and can also help reduce high blood pressure.
Vanilla is a sweet-smelling spice with an intense aroma that is extracted from a specific orchid variety characterized by large yellow flowers. Vanillin, the substance composing it, has antiseptic, digestion-promoting and, according to tradition, aphrodisiac properties. Recently, some studies have demonstrated that it also has an antidepressant action.

1 serving

1 cup (150 g) strawberries
1 lemon

1/3 cup (100 g) dense whole
yogurt (Greek or similar)
3 tbsp. (40 g) whipping cream

STRAWBERRY JUICE AND YOGURT

1. Wash the strawberries under running water, remove the stems and juice half of them in a centrifugal juicer.

2. Place the remaining strawberries to dry on a kitchen towel and then transfer into a bowl.

3. Juice the lemon and filter the juice through a strainer.

4. Using an immersion blender or a whisk, blend the yogurt, cream, lemon juice and strawberry juice. Blend until a homogeneous mixture is obtained. Transfer the mixture into a bowl and flavor with the left over strawberries.

5. Recommended for special occasions, this beverage is rich in flavor and fairly caloric (with respect to fruit and vegetable protein based recipes) and can make an excellent dessert.

Difficulty: MEDIUM
Preparation: **10 minutes**
Calories: **245 kcal**

Recipe Properties:
The Strawberry Juice and Yogurt has an excellent flavor and taste. It is rich in proteins and antioxidants, and has a high satiety index. In addition to protecting the intestine, it also stimulates the nervous and immune systems. It is an excellent beverage for children and adolescents.

Strawberry *protects the body's tissues from aging; it has depurative, flushing and anti-cellulite properties. It contributes to the burning of fats helping to lose weight, and protects teeth from periodontitis and cavities. This fruit contains various compounds that help restore the balance of the central nervous system, and due to its folic acid contents, helps prevent age-related memory loss. Finally, it has been included among the "super foods" for its elevated ("record") contents of beneficial antioxidants.*
Yogurt *actively contributes to child growth due to its contents of the same proteins contained in milk, and has good amounts of zinc, one of the minerals important to skin balance.*

BIOGRAPHIES

Maurizio Cusani, who was born in Como, works as a doctor in Milan. Some years back he developed an interest in nutrition and its effects on human health. To learn more about this new-found interest he became a student of Sufism and ancient traditions, which he has always been particularly interested in on his travels. He teaches classes about the Enneagram and the Symbology of the Human Body to students of Naturopathy and to graduate students of Psychosomatics for Doctors and Psychologists at the Riza Institute. He has written numerous monographs and texts about Nutraceutics, Symbolism, Sufism, Ancient Traditions, Psychosomatics and wellbeing in general. For White Star Publisher, he co-authored *Gluten-Free Gourmet Recipes* and *Fat-Free Gourmet Recipes* with Cinzia Trenchi.

Cinzia Trenchi, naturopath, journalist and freelance photographer specialized in nutrition and wine and food itineraries, has collaborated on numerous recipe books published in Italy and abroad. A passionate cook, she has also been working for many years with different Italian magazines, revisiting specialties of regional, traditional, macrobiotic and natural cuisines, providing text and photographs, and proposing dishes of her own invention. Her cookbooks propose original and creative foods, pairing flavors and trying unusual accompaniments in a search of great-tasting food while keeping the nutritional properties of the ingredients in mind, in order to achieve a balanced diet and the consequent improvement in wellbeing. She lives in a house immersed in greenery in Monferrato, in Piedmont. Using flowers, aromatic herbs and vegetables from her garden, she prepares original sauces and condiments, as well as decorations for dishes, letting herself be guided by the changing of the seasons and by her knowledge of the fruits of the earth. For White Star Publisher, she has published *Gluten-Free Gourmet Recipes, Fat-Free Gourmet Recipes, Chili Pepper - Moments of Spicy Passion* and *My Favorite Recipes*.

INDEX

All photographs are by **Cinzia Trenchi** except the following:
page 1 **haveseen/123RF**
pages 2-3 **saschanti17/Shutterstock**
pages 4-3 **tanjichica/Shutterstock**
illustrations of vegetables and fruit **Siarhei Pleshakov/123RF**
illustrations of organic products **Samtoon/123RF**

EDITORIAL DIRECTOR
VALERIA MANFERTO DE FABIANIS

GRAPHIC DESIGN
PAOLA PIACCO

WHITE STAR PUBLISHERS

WS White Star Publishers® is a registered trademark
property of De Agostini Libri S.p.A.

© 2015 De Agostini Libri S.p.A.
Via G. da Verrazano, 15 - 28100 Novara, Italy
www.whitestar.it - www.deagostini.it

Translation, editing and layout: TperTradurre s.r.l.

ISBN 978-88-544-0938-5
1 2 3 4 5 6   19 18 17 16 15

Printed in Croatia